SOCIETAL *SHIFT*

A WORLD WITHOUT BORDERS
AND A HOME WITHOUT WALLS

OPAL SINGLETON

XP BOOKS

XP BOOKS
2301 Lucien Way #415
Maitland, FL 32751
407.339.4217
www.xulonpress.com

XP
BOOKS

Printed in the United States of America.

ISBN-13: 9781545653135

ENDORSEMENTS

"*Societal Shift* is a must-read. Written by one of the nation's leading experts on human trafficking, sextortion, social media exploitation and child pornography, Opal Singleton pulls back the curtain on a world that is hidden in plain sight. Brace yourself for an education and awareness of a world deserving more attention and response." Opal has carefully interwoven the impact of advancing technologies and crimes against children as six billion people are brought together by the Global Internet. The impact on our society and the next generation is profound. You will find this book to be intriguing, insightful and I assure you, it will disrupt your comfort zone. Every parent and educator in America should read this book.

Dr. Erroll G. Southers

University of Southern California

Sol Price School of Public Policy

Professor of the Practice in National & Homeland Security

Director, Safe Communities Institute

Director, Homegrown Violent Extremism Studies

Director of International Programs (CREATE)

3335 S. Figueroa Street, Unit A

Los Angeles, CA 90089-7273

(213) 740-9961

Website: https://sci.usc.edu

Opal Singleton is a nationally known subject matter expert on advancing technologies and crimes against humanity, especially crimes against children. She is both academia and activist and educates law enforcement, first responders, educators and parents and teens across the nation. You will find this book to be cutting edge, based on thousands of hours of research on how advancing technologies are being used by pedophiles, predators, pimps, cartels and organized crimes to seduce and exploit our teenagers. Opal explores the deep-seated psychological experiences involved in online grooming, internet seduction, fantasy relationships, and the prism of shame when it all goes wrong. This book is gripping, eye opening, and yes, VERY disturbing. I assure you, you will share this book with everyone you know.

Captain Craig Poulson
Los Angeles Fire Leadership Training Academy

Without a doubt, Opal Singleton is one of the most knowledgeable and passionate experts that I know in the fight against human trafficking and the fight for keeping children and vulnerable persons safe from predators. She has devoted extraordinary amounts of time to researching these important and timely topics and educating youth, parents, families, law enforcement and community leaders. I admire her commitment to this cause and trust her expertise. And I'm happy to number her among my friends.

Kerry Decker, Pastor

Compass Christian Church
Riverside California

"Over the past decade, Opal Singleton has been following trends in human trafficking and sextortion cases in order to educate thousands across the country. Not only is she a leading researcher, but she also brings an astonishing amount of heart to her work. This book is no exception--Singleton presents a timely and essential call to action. *A World Without Boarders, A Home Without Walls* is on the cutting edge of presenting and analyzing human trafficking cases. In her book, Singleton examines the dangerous truths of leaving children unattended with access to the Internet through various communication technologies. By exploring the interconnected phenomenon of the "digital age," readers are presented with actual sextortion cases that frequently led to sex trafficking. In addition, readers are taken on a journey through both the positive and negative tensions of social media, trendy applications, and Internet connected video games. In sum, this is an important read and serves as a cautionary reality for past, present, and future generations."

Dr. Julie L. Taylor

Assistant Professor

Department of Communication Studies

California State University, San Bernardino

"Opal Singleton is prophetic in the sense of the Old Testament prophets who served as a guiding light when their people could not discern the threats of society around them, and would wander towards sure destruction. They shouted out and wrote down their warnings for anyone who would listen. As in those times, we now live in a world that is eager to exploit anyone and everyone, including children. But the reach of those who would exploit has been magnified. Adults seem unaware of the ways in which today's predators and traffickers are employing new technologies to multiply their power a thousand-fold to reach children in their very own homes and schools, preying upon the weakest and most vulnerable. Opal Singleton has been tireless in researching in this field and educating anyone and everyone who would listen--teachers, parents, children, social services professionals, law enforcement professionals, etc. Her book is a gift, even more so as readers help in Opal's vision to protect, by sharing it. I am keenly aware that every educator that I reach with what I've learned from Opal, every parent with whom I share her books, may represent one more child who is kept safe."

Ginger Ketting-Weller, PhD

Dean, School of Education

La Sierra University

4500 Riverwalk Parkway

Riverside, CA 92515

E-mail: gkw@lasierra.edu

Telephone: 951-785-2266

DEDICATION

This book is dedicated to my late husband, Del Singleton. He was the light of my life. It was my great fortune to be his wife. His wit, his intelligence, his maturity, his generosity, his insights will often be reflected throughout this book. I believe this may be the most important work I have ever done and I greatly miss having those spontaneous moments, where I would turn suddenly and say "Hey, Babe, what about this?"

Del was one of the finest men I ever met. We met when I was 27 and we were together for 44 incredible years. For the first time in my life, I had someone who believed in me. In fact, it was Del that taught me that the most important four words in life are "I believe in

You!". And when those four words come from strong moral males, with good boundaries, it will change the life of women and girls around them.

Del left an incredible legacy as a man who believed in others. It was that understanding of how we all want someone to believe in us that helped me comprehend why so many young people around the world fall prey as they are desperately seeking someone to believe in them. I dedicate this book to Del Singleton. I know if he were here, he would say "Never Again" should another man, woman, or child be violated because they wanted to be loved.

I also dedicate this book to the men and women of RCAHT, The Riverside County Anti Human Trafficking Task Force. Certainly, I am prejudiced; I don't apologize. They are the best of the best, taking on the worst of the worst. They are dedicated men and women who spend endless hours listening to cell phone conversations, building cases, going under- cover, conducting investigations to get some of the vilest people on earth, people who sell other peo- ple's bodies and especially when they sell the body is a child.

RCAHT has allowed me to be their public speaker for several years. It is by far one of the most unique relationships you can imagine. That is something only God could have arranged. It has been my pleasure and privilege to work with them and I will be forever grateful that God opened this door. I have learned so much from them about how predators operate, and I have diligently tried to share that information with thousands of people so we are informed and can protect our families. It takes a unique individual that can get up every morning and face the world of sex trafficking. Sgt. John Sawyer and the men and women of RCAHT are my heroes. These are true champions who go far beyond the call of duty to make sure kids won't be violated. I count them as my friends.

I also want to thank Susie Carpenter who is Million Kids' Media and Marketing Director. She just might be the most talented person on earth for social media marketing and graphic arts. Everyone who works with Million Kids has a "paying job" in addition to what they do for Million Kids. For Susie, it is Amazon. She posts many of the stories to Million Kids website on her break. She is amazing. She has extraordinary talent and a heart of gold for kids who are exploited. Thank you, Susie. She is truly the face of Million Kids.

I also want to thank Mona Lumpkin, Million Kids Administrative Assistant. When I lost my husband, she stepped in and picked up the pieces. She is the backbone of the "business part" of Million Kids. As she will tell you, I have many talents but organization and operating technology are not part of them. She fixes it when it is broken and I could not make all of this happen without her.

I would like to give a special shout out to Dr. Erroll Southers of USC Sol Price School of Safe Communities and Captain Craig Poulson of the Los Angeles Fire Leadership Training Academy. These exceptional leaders have exhibited cutting edge leadership in creating world class education programs for law enforcement, fire departments, code enforcement, public safety administrators, port authority, and social service providers across the nation. It has been my unique privilege to provide the curriculum and training on human trafficking, sextortion, social media exploitation, and child pornography to an elite group of first responders enrolled in their programs. It is the give and take from their participants that validate and guide my research and prepare the next generation of leadership and administrators to combat these horrific crimes across the U.S.

Thank you to the many donors to Million Kids. The list is made up of incredible people who may not be wealthy but dig into their pockets each month so they can change a child's life. We could not do that without you. Let me name a few: Hillside, Calvary Chapel, Williams, Edelbrock, Poulson, Skip & Friends Church, Deets, Singleton, Compass Christian Church, Smith, Drachand, Beck, Ford, Weller, Flores, Rising, Arnold, Strickland, Soroptimists, Southhills, Lexis Nexis, Refuge, Impact Club, Anderson, BMW Riverside, Horgan, Railsback, Protz, Conner, Marshall, Pacillas, Purvis, Fraser, Duvivier, Savage, Kuehne, Parker, Lee, Gaylor, Taylor, Gordon, Reliance, Thompson, Voll, Stickel, McArdell, Mountry, Efurd, Auburn, Casida, Schmidt, West, Rose, Polos, Whitaker, Bonczewski, Martinez, Rush, Gutman, Hunt, Pendergraft, Kurey, Rumbel, Alavi, Balough, Ursel, Hergenreder, Dowd, Orate, Pechanga, Kidby, Graham, Uplanders Club, Barnabas and many more. If you donated and I did not acknowledge you, please know that you ARE important to me. Thank you from the bottom of my heart. Without you we cannot make this happen.

I want to say thank you to my personal counselor Claudia Bouslough. You cannot survive in this business without personal counseling and she is the best. Week after week, she hears me out without judging me. Thank you for letting me purge my soul so I can do this work. I also want to say thank you to Kerry Decker who started Million Kids in 2008 and later entrusted me with it. His artistic talent has been critical in helping Million Kids help others. And finally, thank you to my home church, Compass Christian Church in Riverside. They are my family. I can simply go in and disappear as I turn my ragged soul over to my Higher Power. They save my place so I know I am home.

This business is a tough business. Especially without the companionship and support of my incredible husband, I never dreamed I would find myself here in my retirement. But once you have sat with the parent of a violated child or sat with a child who is being blackmailed, you simply cannot look back. I am only able to do this work by the Grace of God. Thank You.

FOREWARD

I t is almost here! The year 2020 is predicted to be one of the most historic eras in human history as literally SIX BILLION people are joined together around the globe via the Internet. This has never happened before. Our society seems capable of absorbing and adapting to new technologies on a daily basis; but, few of us are looking at the impact it will have on our young people, our families and the moral foundations for our society.

Opal Singleton has conducted thousands of hours of research on the impact of advancing technologies and how those technologies will change crime and crime solving. Even more importantly, is how those technologies will change families, social and moral values and even more deep-seated issues such as self-perception and self-worth. As Opal points out in this book, it is truly the greatest societal experiment in history.

As the Global Outreach Pastor of a very large Church located in Southern California, I share the concerns that Opal is addressing in this book. I have spent 20 years visiting over 70 nations around the world and have seen first-hand how impoverished and displaced people have increasingly become vulnerable victims to human traffickers. I now spend the majority of my time working with children in Foster Care system as they are the most vulnerable to victimizers in my local community. Today, those traffickers and victimizers do not even need to travel to foreign lands as those vulnerable people and even their innocent children can be reached by technology. In fact, in almost every culture it is the young people who are the FIRST to gain access to technology and sadly many of their parents are the last to understand the dangers that technology is presenting to their children. Compounding that crisis is the idea that is held by many young people, that their behavior in the virtual world of technology and gaming holds no real-life consequences and this concept makes them especially vulnerable to the exploitative traps of online victimizers.

As leaders in our communities facing the challenge of this next chapter in human history, we must work to understand the opportunities these developing technologies provide and most especially the dangers those very same technologies present to the most vulnerable amongst us such as the impoverished, the displaced and our innocent children. Opal writes extensively on these topics to help us gain that understanding and insight.

Opal does an incredible job laying out all of these challenges in her book. She helps us to understand how the victimizers utilize seemingly innocent aspects of current and developing technology in ways that create a lifetime of harm to their victims and how we can work to prevent the vulnerable from becoming victims. Opal presents real life cases that serve to give us insight into the layers of shame and suffering victimizers heap onto their victims even through virtual online relationships which enables us to come alongside the victims and restore them back to wholeness and healing. Every person can benefit from Opal's many years of work in the challenging field of anti-human trafficking and the compassion with which she equips us to prevent and restore victims in the future. This book is a MUST READ for every concerned parent, community leader and societal change agent.

Reverend Dr. Skip Lanfried
Friends Church
Yorba Linda, California

PREFACE

"**G**RANDMA: "I know everything, just not all the time." Those are the words of my five-year-old granddaughter. God must rejoice at the innocence of a child. It seems to be a lost art. Believe me, an innocent child is a work of art: rare and joyful and something to be cherished.

This is the most important (and vulnerable) generation that has ever walked the face of the earth. I believe the world is an extraordinary place to live and that we live in historic times.

Despite the politics, terrorism, global warming, cyber-crime, hacking, and on and on, our lives are infinitely more comfortable and luxurious than any generation before us. We can instantly communicate around the globe, sending photos and live streaming, sharing emotions with millions of people we have never met. That also means millions of people will share with us. There will be more information and personal opinions, ideologies and propaganda available to us and our children than at any time in history. But it comes with no barometer, no truth measure to determine what is real and what is suspicious or even deliberately altered to manipulate and indoctrinate our innocent minds.

Every generation before us has said that the "next generation is going to hell in a handbasket". As people get older, they become depressed at the way the world is changing and for many it seems things are getting worse. I have often thought it was because it is difficult for older people to adapt to change and therefore, they become judgmental of what they cannot participate in. I have tried not to be one of "THOSE" people.

However, it is a fact that over the past decade there has been a world-wide effort to liberalize sexual attitudes and moral standards. There seems to be a concerted effort to corrupt any sense of decorum or decency. When nine-year-olds are twerking naked on live streaming and the children's movie "Angry Birds" contains the "F" word over and over, you cannot help but wonder where these changes are going. I always experience a sense of loss over each of these events as I cannot see the good in them. The child is not achieving, growing emotionally or spiritually or even intellectually. In fact, we are paving the way for children to compromise their own souls, their sense of worth and value, all in the name of wanting to remain loved and approved of.

Of primary concern to me is that as I have witnessed young people continuously lower their moral expectations and standards, they increasingly become more vulnerable to being exploited and violated by predators and organized crime. Pimps and pedophiles quickly surmise which kids are willing to take a chance or walk on the wild side and throw caution to the wind. We all make mistakes and each and every one of us has compromised ourselves in some way. What I fear is that without a moral compass or truth barometer, many young people will live a life of compromise and simply accept that they are damaged goods. They will accept exploitation from others because they believe that is all they are worth. That self-assessment makes them infinitely more vulnerable to be preyed on by exploiters.

Time and time again in this book you will be a witness to how this plays out. I work with parents who are trying desperately to keep their child from committing one of the biggest mistakes of their lives: running off with some low life guy or girl they have developed a fantasy relationship with.

Too many times, I have heard the heartache and sobbing of a father as he experiences the loss of innocence of his teenage daughter who has unwittingly allowed herself to be seduced or coerced into activities that result in violation or exploitation by an online predator or by a pimp boyfriend that is trying to snatch her away from her family. It is truly gut-wrenching.

Throughout this book you will hear me reiterate that technology is not good or bad. I love technology and believe our children's lives will ultimately be much the better for it. What is a concern is that the great societal experiment we are living in comes with no instructions.

I believe that a large segment of our young kids will survive this societal experiment with minimal damage. For sure, they will try out some risky behaviors and be exposed to a great deal of sexual information that most of us would find appalling. But they will survive. Some will not be so fortunate. We are playing roulette with this generation as day after day, new apps, technologies, video games, live streaming etc. are introduced WITHOUT

INSTRUCTIONS OR WARNING on how they could be used to violate a young person.

It is an interesting situation. Whenever there is an advertisement of a pharmaceutical drug on television, they go through elaborate warnings. "This little blue pill is going to make you happy, and relieve your anxiety, however, your toenails may turn green, your hair will fall out and a small percentage of you may "die" but you will have found "The cure" for your depression." Think about it. Even criminals are warned they have a right to remain silent because what they say can and will be used against them. So where are the warnings for apps, chat rooms and new technologies that can and will be used by pedophiles and pimps to exploit our children? Where are the instructions or warnings of the dangers for our kids?

Few leaders are talking about this. It is as if our world has decided that if we don't mention it, maybe it won't happen to OUR child. Perhaps there is a fear of being labeled an extremist or a kook, or out of touch. Truthfully, I sit with parents whose child has been violated and I work with kids who are being blackmailed, sextorted and bullied. Once you have sat with one of these victims of exploitation, you simply cannot look back. Label me whatever you want, but SOMEONE has to help these folks and SOMEONE needs to call it what it is--social media exploitation, sex trafficking, sextortion, child pornography. Each can destroy a beautiful, innocent soul. That is what this book is about!

INTRODUCTION

SOCIETAL SHIFT: A WORLD WITHOUT BORDERS, A HOME WITHOUT WALLS

W e live at one of the most unique times in all of history: Maybe THE most unique time. Perhaps the trilogy of **Global Refugee and Immigration, Terrorism and Home-Grown Violent Extremism, Technology and Global Internet Connection** are even more important than the Industrial Revolution.

What an amazing time to be alive! Certainly, there have been many times throughout history where entire societies and cultures were altered. I think of the Renaissance and the Dark Ages. In more current times, the devastating impact of World War II and the Holocaust and the Khmer Rouge changed societies worldwide. There have been times of surging growth and wealth. Advances in technologies such as electricity and the combustion engine automobile changed day-to-day life dramatically. Telecommunications have brought people together. Broadcasts of news and foreign affairs from far away countries are received in a matter of minutes instead of weeks and months.

There are three defining factors for this historic period.

Global Refugee and Immigration:

Globally, we are seeing millions of refugees and displaced people losing their entire fortunes, their income, their livelihood, their stability, their dignity. A homeless person is an EXPLOITED person. As I write this, tens of thousands of migrants and refugees are beginning their journey through the Balkans to arrive in communities where they are not welcome. Millions of displaced people from Syria, Afghanistan and Kosovo are trying to find a new home in foreign lands. European cities like Belgrade, Macedonia, Rome, London, Paris, Athens struggle to accommodate millions of people with no source of income and little stability while it changes the cultural and economic landscape of their once placid lifestyle.

The New York Times reports that tens of thousands of migrants from poor African nations are arriving by boat, land, and air into Europe. Poverty and war in places like Libya, South Sudan, Eritrea and Nigeria are driving migrants to make the perilous journey across the Mediterranean Sea. The tidal wave of desperate human beings is so overwhelming that European leaders said they would form a naval force based in Italy to combat people-smuggling. Entire cities like Paris, Munich, and London, struggle to maintain their deeply engrained cultural history as the ethnicities of their populations ebb and flow. It is believed that more than a million displaced Ukrainians have fled to Russia. And in a lesser known but severely exploitive situation, is the plight of thousands of Bangladeshis and Rohingya, an ethnic minority from Myanmar, that have fled from poverty and persecution into the borders of Thailand.

Some have set up "homes" in the trash dumps of Mae Sot. (if you want to help them go to MillionKids.org)

The United States is no exception although it is not as obvious as to what is going on in Europe. The past ten years have brought changes in interpretation of immigration laws that have allowed literally millions to migrate from Latin and South America, many with no documentation. As total societies are taken over by cartels, people flee northward in hopes of finding a safe place to raise their family. Drug cartels have replaced elected politicians and in societies like El Salvador, whole cities are controlled by MS-13. We hear of ISIS style beheadings in Mexico and just recently, the poverty rate reached new highs in Venezuela as the government turned to Bitcoin to stabilize their national currency. Today, the U.S. Census Bureau reports that in California, 49% of households speak a language other than English at home.

Why does this matter in the discussion of "Societal Shift"? It is because a displaced person is a desperate person, willing to take risks to find a new life. They will pursue job offers even though they know in their heart of hearts the job is too good to be true.

They will compromise, hoping against hope this might work out OK for them and their families. Displaced persons will take chances they never would have taken in their previous situation. And there are those scoundrels and opportunists that will travel with them that will prey on their compromised circumstances. Woven within every society are good people and evil people.

What we are witnessing in this decade are thousands of people who now can be accessed through technology by total strangers they have never met, or local recruiters promising jobs in a far-off land that will help them build a new life. Some of these victims pay $5000 to $8000 for these new "jobs". When they arrive at their destination, they find they are not going to be a welder, a construction worker, a truck driver, a nanny, a food server, a housekeeper, but they are going to be forced into commercial sex, twenty hours a day, servicing more than ten clients a day and they will never get to keep ANY of the money that is collected through their exploitation. Or they will find that instead of a welding job, they are working in the back of a restaurant or care home twenty hours a day. When it is time to get paid, 80% of their income is deducted for "room and board". This entrapment is called HUMAN TRAFFICKING and it is the fastest growing illegal enterprise in the world.

2.) Terrorism and Home-Grown Violent Extremism

It seems like at least once a week the world hears about another bombing or speeding car plowing into a crowd of people. We all wait and wonder if this is the work of ISIS or a deranged individual with some radical ideology we have not yet heard of. Our lives have changed and it is unsettling.

The insidious nature of these events is that even though we and our loved ones are not the direct target of the event, we are ALL victimized.

Terrorism and Home-Grown Violent Extremism are 21st century phenomena that disrupt our sense of PREDICTABILITY.

Most of us live our lives with a sense of order, a feeble attempt at believing we are in control of our lives. We plan, we strategize, we dream and we move forward with a sense of safety and being able to manage and yes, even control the everyday elements of our lives. But terrorism by its very nature is designed to rob all of us of that sense of order. Terrorism reminds us that a person (or persons) we have never met can change our lives. In this era, we are all acutely aware that if we go to a mall, a rock festival, a ball game, a marathon, our work place, or even have a latte at a neighborhood café, we could become the victim of violence.

It really is the cumulative effect of individuals with extreme ideologies who have been relocated into global societies combined with access and influence provided through social media that is the pivotal point for this "Societal Shift". We have the confluence, the intersect, of outside forces far beyond our control, that are setting the stage for a society with greater influence on individuals and the family in a way we have never before experienced in all of history.

3.) Technology and Global Internet Connection

The biggest influencing factor in the "Societal Shift" is exploding technology. For the first time in all of history, the entire world will be connected by Internet allowing communications far beyond our ability to imagine even three years ago. Today, in a poor developing country like Cambodia, half of the residents have access to some sort of communications technology. Certainly, it is not an iPhone. In countries like Cambodia it is called "same, same but different" referring to cheap knock off phones of the original. But still, it allows access to the outside world never before experienced in all of history.

This is a true game changer. On the up side of things, just imagine what is possible. Today, the poorest child in the entire world can get an education equivalent to Harvard if they desire and are able access the Internet. People, who were held back because they could not speak English, can learn English by accessing the Internet.

Young people today will have careers we cannot even fathom at this time. Entire new industries will open up based on ever changing technologies like disappearing video, encrypted messaging, live streaming, virtual reality, crypto currency and global cyber sexual exploitation. Communications are changing as information is no longer limited to the top three local TV channels or even the 24-hour news cycle. Today, we are inundated with blogs, podcasts, and customized advertising based on our personal interests and immediate photos instantly submitted within seconds of the latest terrorist attack, wildfire or hurricane disaster.

On the down side, it is estimated that 87% of teenagers sleep with their phones. That means it is truly a "HOME WITHOUT WALLS". At any given time, our kids can be accessed by millions of pedophiles and predators around the world. And if they are sleeping with their phone, that means they can be reached at 3 AM, in the safety of their bed within the walls of their home (sanctuary) in their underwear or jammies. Total strangers can come into their lives and connect with them in the most intimate way.

This trilogy--Global Migration, Terrorism and Homegrown Violent Extremism, and Evolving Technologies connecting the entire globe-- places us all smack dab in the middle of a chaotic and accelerating society. There are no rule books for these phenomena. Parents are caught totally unprepared as teenagers are by nature technology wizards and most parents and grandparents are techno phobic and some are techno impotent.

There has probably never been a more challenging time to be a parent. Today, total strangers are able to access, groom, recruit, and exploit our young people. Today, total strangers can chat with your child (sometimes for hours in video game chat rooms) about things like spirituality, morality and sexuality, even gender choice, and ISIS. These were thought to be the "Holy Grail" for parents just a few short months ago. As many of you are aware, I wrote my first book on this subject "Seduced: The Grooming of America's Teenagers". (You can go to WWW.MillionKids.org to order).

For most, we will all adapt and survive and yes, maybe reluctantly, most will thrive. We will adjust.

However, for some, these factors are catastrophic. I believe that today it is possible that for most young people, their first sexual experience will be a 'VIRTUAL SEXUAL" experience. Many of our precious guys and girls will be sextorted (blackmailed) because they trusted their new online friend and sent them a naked photo.

Nearly once or twice a week we hear of a 14-year-old, straight A student, a beautiful girl with two loving parents living in the lap of luxury, who decides to sneak out of the house and meet up with her new-found love on the internet. By the time she is in the car and realizes he is not "a hot rock star" but rather more like Frankenstein, it is simply too late.

As we progress through this book, we will explore the wide range of impacts this trilogy will have on our lives. We will look at challenges to crime and crime solving. We will look at how the psychology of grooming takes place. We will explore "phantom relationships" where a total stranger, someone they will never meet, can come into our kid's lives and get them to commit vile sex acts on themselves and film it and share it and in some cases even commit suicide. We will look at "WHY" people try to trick our kids into sending naked photos and just where do those photos really go. Most important, we will discuss tactics, strategies, parenting skills, and legislation activity that might be a solution to keeping our kids safe from predators.

TABLE OF CONTENTS

CHAPTER ONE:

CYBER FANTASY

W e are entering one of the greatest societal experiments in history. It is an interesting situation how cyberspace changes our perception of reality. Time after time we see people do and say things on the Internet they would normally never do and say in different circumstances. If you think I am wrong, simply Google YouTube and search for the word "Omegle". You will find video after video of America's teenagers sitting in their own bedrooms exhibiting some of the most bizarre behavior you can image with total strangers on the screen. Presumably, Mom or Dad is at the grocery store and have no conscious understanding of the extreme behavior a teenager will tryout with a total stranger.

Adults are not exempt either. Cyberspace makes us feel as if we have entered <u>a world without consequences.</u> I think of Anthony Weiner. Love him or hate him, here is a man who had attained some level of public accomplishment but could not resist sending photos of his phallic symbol to minors. Surely a man with his education and intelligence could have perceived the reality of where those photos might end up, but he simply could not stop. And of course, it destroyed him and his reputation. There is seemingly no obvious quid pro quo in cyberspace, no ability to visualize cause and effect. The simple reality that "if I do this", then there will be consequences which could be quite costly.

Once you realize how that plays out for adults, then it is easier to understand how quickly an unsophisticated teenager who is hormonal and seeking to "hook up" can be ensnared. Many teenagers have told me that what they do on the Internet does not count because it is not "real".

I believe most of us have sat at a keyboard, or sent a tweet, email or photo that we have regretted.

Cyberspace is the world's billboard. Nothing has prepared the average adult or child on how quickly a post, tweet, photo can go viral.

One of the reasons it is such a challenge is that cyberspace came with no instruction manual. Only after lives are destroyed by a naked photo or a child is exploited by a casual hookup with a person met on the Internet do we learn that perhaps, if used inappropriately, technology can be dangerous. That is when I get involved as President of Million Kids. Some weeks I receive six, eight, ten cases where eleven-year-old girls and sixteen-year-old boys have been horribly psychologically violated and some physically raped.

In the meantime, we are putting children on the WORLD WIDE WEB in vast numbers and they are younger and younger. Cyberspace is truly the coming together of our society. ALL of it: Both the good and the bad. Somehow parents are unable to visualize the reality of that statement that cyberspace has connected all of us. Just possibly the lab animals we are experimenting with, in this case, are our kids. It just may be the greatest societal experiment of all time.

Think about this, as the world is connected by technology, there will be at least SIX BILLION people online. Let's suppose only 1% of them are bad guys, you know, like pedophiles, rapists, child pornographers, money launderers, sex traffickers, Satanists, terrorists, etc. That would mean a world where you and your child are entering a community of <u>60 million bad guys</u> (and women). I would agree that you and your child will not be exposed to all 60 million pedophiles but let's say they can be accessed by 1% of them. That is still 600,000 pedophiles that are seeking a child they can befriend, lure in and exploit. We are playing roulette with our children and ourselves.

It is almost like there is a cyber veil from reality. We are unable to bring ourselves to comprehend the possibility. Most of us would never take a 7-8-9-year-old child or even a pre-pubescent child down to a strip club and leave them off for an hour or so to see how they are able to negotiate with sophisticated exploiters. When we are able to visualize that scenario, we all think how ridiculous it is. No child, even if they are the most brilliant child on earth, has the judgement or sexual knowledge to stand against

4

hundreds of experienced and sophisticated predators with years of expertise in how to seduce and
exploit a child. And yet, somehow, we think our child
will be exceptional and they will be OK on the Internet.

I will share with you a typical example of how this
plays out. I read a case of a nine-year-old boy who
was apparently brilliant beyond his years and super
intelligent. So, Mom and Dad gave him a smart phone.
He immediately uploaded Kik, the instant messaging
app. How he knows about the app Kik I am not sure,
but it does tell you what a nine-year-old knows and
we old codgers do not!

Maybe, he knew about it from a friend. He immediately was able to find a new "friend" and hook up.
Unfortunately, it was a 44-year-old pedophile and
they struck up a conversation. This same young man
would never arbitrarily talk to a stranger in person
but this is the world of cyber fantasy where talking to
strangers is not only OK but desired. After a while the
man talked him into removing his clothes and filming
himself partially naked.

Perhaps he just wanted to impress his new friend
with how technologically savvy he was. At nine I doubt
that he understood why a 44-year-old man wants a

photo of a naked little boy. Either way, he wanted to please him and he did.

The reason we know about this incident is that the parents that evening saw a strange man sitting outside their home watching their son playing in the back yard and called the police. As the police searched the man's phone they found the photo. What the boy did not realize is that unless you disable it, photos have GPS attached to them. Once the pedophile received the naked photo, he was able to determine where the child lived. Even more disturbing is that the pedophile had most likely sold that photo of the naked boy over and over, thousands of times in the Dark Net to other pedophiles.

One of the unique phenomena about social media is its ability to bring the whole world together while creating an environment that "feels" like fantasy. As we previously mentioned, kids will tell you that what they do on the Internet does not count because it is cyberspace and not reality. The cyber community seems to take on a life and importance of its own. It seems to transcend normal family values and influence when a child is evaluating interactions and trust in relationships on the Internet.

Time and time again you will see families at dinner, everyone including Mom and Dad texting and tweeting without even looking at each other. I saw this play out in the saddest way one day. I was having breakfast at Mimi's on a casual Saturday morning. The family next to me was obviously celebrating Grandma's birthday. There were six adults, most likely her adult kids, and two older teens. The eight of them sat there totally engaged in their phones. These folks appeared to be normal professional people who would never be rude or impolite. They most likely were not even cognizant of their own behavior. I doubt that they actually said ten whole words to Grandma. You could see her trying to be polite and engage but after a while her demeanor changed as she realized they did not even acknowledge her presence. It could be my imagination but I could almost see her starting to re-write her will right there at the breakfast table.

Two things are obvious about social media and the social validation feedback loop. They not only allow you to be self-absorbed but self-absorption becomes the primary behavioral modification. Much has been written about social media and technology addiction. I don't believe we need a scientific pontification for all of us to agree that most of us are addicted. It is all about ME and my needs.

This truth was really driven home to me one morning in church. Keep in mind, I wrote a book on social media and fantasy relationships: *Seduced: The Grooming of America's Teenagers*. Even though I understand it completely, I am no different than anyone else. Here I was sitting in church and the minister was preaching. I felt my phone vibrate. I was like Pavlov's dog, wanting to check and see who wanted my feedback or if maybe someone might need me. Here I was worshipping God and yet, even though I am an expert on the subject, I could hardly resist the urge to check my phone. It is all about ME.

Social media not only changes relationships, it changes the family dynamic. The family must decide deliberately that it will not change their interactions. For many who live and breathe in the alter world of cyberspace, actual family interaction is an intrusion. It is perceived as something that must be tolerated until they can get back to the "Real" world of online game chat rooms, Instagram or Snapchat.

One of the good potential things about social media is that it CAN change the family dynamic to the better because they can communicate more often since it is convenient. But there is a difference between communicating and engaging. It is critical to understand the difference.

The world of social media will communicate a plethora of facts through texts, emojis, likes, posts and comments but the communication is often devoid of emotions and intimacy. Engagement means taking the time to stop your world and connect on a deeper level with the other person's reality whether it is joy, pain, fear, intimacy etc. There is an exchange of emotions. This allows both parties the time and connection to bond, to build trust and evaluate another human being based on the five senses of touch, feel, smell, hearing and sight. Texting with one's thumbs can obviously communicate significant details of our daily lives, but all of us are human beings who respond best to real life interaction.

The reason I call this the greatest societal experiment of all time is that this is not reversible. Our world is hurling forward into new technologies at the speed of light. There is no looking back and I would not want to. As parents we must adapt. This is truly the most historical era of all time. I often say it may be even more important than the Industrial Revolution. This is also the most challenging time of all times to be a parent.

Technology can and will be our greatest friend if we decide. But we MUST DECIDE. It must be a strategy. And frankly parents, it must be a strategy that husband and wife and yes, ex-husband and ex-wife must decide together. There should not be an ounce of daylight between you or your child's life can be changed forever.

Parents need to understand the universe we live in, identify the good and the bad, and pick your challenges and your battle lines. I believe in starting with the positive. BEFORE your child gets a phone. However, this is getting harder and harder because I see little kids 4, 5, 6-year-olds playing video games. And I wonder if the parents really understand the entire Internet world they are setting that child up for.

It is a fascinating thing to me. We would never give a nine-year-old a loaded gun and have them carry it all day. We would not give them the keys to the car until they have completed drivers ed. We would not hand them a bottle of vodka and tell them to carry it around until they are fourteen but don't open it. And yet time and time again, we turn a blind eye to the reality of technology and think our child will be the exception.

At the risk of sounding like a nut, let me take this a bit further. Some days as I take leads from distraught parents whose children have been violated, I get a different image in my head. It is almost like parents have decided to LET their children play on the freeway because everyone else is doing it and it is the responsibility of the drivers to avoid hitting them. In fact, in the parallel analogy, many parents would not only blame the drivers, they would blame the freeway! And determine that it is Cal Trans fault if their child is violated. Really? Who put them on the freeway in the first place? But I digress.

Recognizing the dangers, let's talk about the up side. This generation will have access to more knowledge than any generation in history. What an extraordinary advantage. Even the poorest child around the globe can learn foreign languages and have access to extraordinary libraries of knowledge if they choose to take advantage of the greatest body of information available in history. They don't have to wait to go to medical school to learn the most intricate details of the physical body. If they want to be a lawyer, they can monitor both sides of an argument as a case plays out around the globe getting input from some of the most brilliant minds in the world. Church youth groups can connect with the mission fields around the globe and teach their students to become cyber missionaries. They can interact with the people they are helping, teach them English, and monitor missions projects half way around the globe.

It is a fascinating phenomenon to me that when the world is handed technologies like live streaming, artificial intelligence, virtual reality, it is often used for evil first. Later, good people figure out that they have a tremendous opportunity to use it to enhance a child's life, to assist the poor, to help the elderly, and to prepare the next generation to become the leaders of safe and empowering technologies for generations to come. That possibility could be greatest challenge of this decade.

I believe with all my heart that we have entered the era of strategic parenting. We can no longer just want to raise healthy and happy children and consider that success. We have entered the era where the whole world is connected and it will change everything that is and was familiar to us. We must not only adapt. We must prepare. We as parents need to make deliberate and well thought out strategies so that our children are prepared for the evolving and expanding global era of being cyber connected. This preparation will not happen by accident.

One of the greatest challenges for parents in this era is that the cyber world and cyber fantasy can replace most of the impact of parents unless parents inform themselves and decide on a course of action where they take the leadership role.

In many cases, once the child receives the phone or computer, it opens the door to the outside world. Truly, it allows total strangers to influence and share ideologies and sexual concepts with our young people. The technology world provides literally thousands of tweets, "YouTube", videos, live streaming, and video game chat room experiences where outside individuals are helping your child formulate attitudes on sexuality, morality, and spirituality. This is the first time in history where our children will be subjected to millions of outside influences even within the confines of their own home. This is why I say. "It is a world without borders and a home without walls".

CHAPTER TWO:

THE GREAT CONUNDRUM- WHEN NINE-YEAR- OLDS' 'TWERK"

**Go to "YouTube". Put in "Live.Me"
Twerking. Brace Yourself!**

I will warn you this chapter is going to be a tough chapter to read. Truthfully, it is a challenging chapter to write. Buckle up. This is meant to be a dialogue, not a statement of my beliefs on this issue. Like everyone else in society, we are still sorting through the short and long-term implications of specific technologies and what it will mean to our kid's safety and to building a moral foundation within our children.

First, let me reiterate (as I do throughout this book). Technology is not bad. In fact, technology is completely revolutionizing our lives, mostly to the good. I think this is one of the most exciting times in all of history to be alive. Today technology comes at us at such a head spinning speed that most of us cannot be sure what it all means or how it affects our lives. People, a lot smarter than me, have written books about 2030, 2050 and beyond and technology. This is not one of those books.

The purpose of this book is to help parents, teachers, leaders, teens, and anyone who is willing to stop and consider the historical impact that technology will have on our society today and for generations to come. As in most things good, there is a down side. The reality of this "Societal Shift" is that in the daily onslaught of new technologies, a portion of our children, teens, and even adults will end up being violated. It is my mission that the more we can understand and prepare others for the potential negative impact of the "Societal Shift", the greater the opportunity for building leadership that is self -responsible and laying the foundation for keeping young people safe from digital predators for generations to come.

One of the phenomena of new technologies is that no one can predict exactly how the pedophile/predator will use it to violate a child. It is people like me who research and study actual cases to glean criminal conduct on new technologies. I then try to warn leadership, law enforcement, and parents quickly of these cases. That is one of the purposes of Million Kids Facebook page. Susie Carpenter, our Media and Marketing Director, researches and posts new cases several times a day. Unfortunately, while this gives us information to globally disperse, it also means that one or several children will have been horribly violated before we can discern how predators are able to use the technology inappropriately and before we can share it with others.

This line of thinking all started for me as I began to review cases of a live streaming app, called Live. Me. They also own Twitch TV. At this writing Live.Me has over 100 million users and is growing rapidly. The app is somewhat unique in that it allows anyone and everyone to live stream whatever they want. Yes, the app has places you have to agree you are an adult and there is a mild general warning about illicit behavior.

Truthfully, the Live.Me app is just the beginning of how social media interaction will take place. By the time this book is in print for a couple of years, I suspect this technology will be so main stream, few of us will think through the long-term implications.

Live.Me combines many features that assist a live streaming performer to generate an audience, experience interaction, and receive feedback from their viewers. Live.Me has a geo function so it promotes your transmission while it is taking place, giving priority to those closest to your geographic location. The viewers can interact with the performer. Live.Me provides "virtual currency" so viewers can reward the performer for particular performances and use it as incentives to get them to increase the intensity or tantalization of a particular performance. I suppose if we were all adults, there would be no issue with this.

However, when you go to YouTube and plug in Live.Me and select the videos where performers are "Twerking" you will see how quickly this can go wrong. So, for you "old fogies" out there that are not aware of "Twerking", let me give you a heads up before you wander into the more salacious edge of our society.

The Merriam Webster Dictionary defines "Twerking" as "sexually suggestive dancing characterized by rapid, repeated hip thrusts and shaking of the buttocks especially while squatting. A Quote from Luke O'Neill defines it a bit differently. "Twerking has become a catch-all for an overtly sexualized style of dancing wherein one manipulates the hips and posterior in an often hypnotic and physics-defying bounce". Let me issue a word of precaution to anyone reading this book who is over forty. If you try to twerk, you may need a chiropractor. If you are over seventy and try to twerk, you may need an ambulance. Twerking is a young person's sport. Thank you, Miley Cyrus.

We are entering a world where no one has ever gone before. There are no rules. There are no instructions. Everyone points the finger at someone else. I have felt for a long time now that part of the consequences of the great "Societal Shift" will mean that a percentage, a portion, some number of young people in our society will be exploited, sexually abused, blackmailed, raped, or violated in some manner because they made themselves available to pedophiles on the Internet.

It is like we have made an unconscious decision or there is at least some level of acceptance by our society that it is inevitable that SOME of our kids will be accessed or exploited by pedophiles. We all want to believe it will be someone else's kid as our kid is smarter, brighter, more sophisticated, more mature than others. It is a game of roulette we are playing with this (and future) generations of young people. Many of our young people will survive it and be fine. Others will not be so lucky and the virtual violation and in many cases the ultimate physical violation will change these young people's lives FOREVER.

I have spent hours on figuring out who is to blame. How does it happen? How can we change it?

Of course, we all start with the perpetrator and I am no exception. Certainly, pedophiles are bad people. Totally evil. The worst of the worst. We KNOW they roam the Internet.

Perhaps parents are not aware of how many there are. Perhaps parents are not educated to understand how they work. Perhaps society needs to find better ways of locking up pedophiles for a long time or providing psychological assistance to pedophiles.

Then there is the challenge that a pedophile cannot ask for help without being reported to law enforcement immediately. It is the responsibility of Mandated Reporters to report anyone admitting to harming a child. So even if they wanted to ask for help, most will not because it is easier to hide in the shadows than risk public shame and incarceration.

Truthfully, it seems that most pedophiles can't be fixed. As least that is the general consensus of professionals who work with pedophilia. I always struggle with that. Maybe it is the Pollyanna in me (we all have some). I would like to believe that if we could reach pedophiles who are only collecting illicit photos without manufacturing or distributing them, perhaps, just maybe we could help them to not offend and save a child from suffering and violation.

I think more research needs to be done on that issue. With existing law making it so a pedophile cannot admit to a therapist about their interest in children without being reported, it will be a hard program to administer. Most professionals who work with pedophiles do not agree with me and I must give them priority because of their many hours of experience and research. I am always looking for some way to save a child from sexual exploitation and there is some remote hope in my heart that if we could catch them early and get them help, maybe another child would be saved.

Most pedophiles are repeat offenders. Over and over, they reoffend. With all the research I have conducted, it appears that they not only reoffend, they escalate their level of violence and humiliation to the victim. Sometimes it ends in death for the victim. At the end of the day, the bottom line is that all of us have to understand that pedophiles exist and that they will do whatever they have to do to access our children. The World Wide Web is their playground and to deny that is folly.

It is my observation that the coming together of the entire world on the Internet will greatly accelerate pedophilia. It is a unique phenomenon that I have been following for many years. It seems that once pedophiles find others in the Clear Web, they realize they share a particular ideology or a specific fetish and that seems to not only legitimize the appropriateness in their mind but actually accelerates their willingness to go far outside the bounds of normality. We will explore this further in Chapter 11: *Global Dark Net and Child Pornography Rings.*

Think about this, prior to social media, a pedophile would find a child and violate them and film it. Perhaps they found another pedophile whom they could share photos. But for the most part, pedophiles kept it to themselves and stayed in the shadows so they would not get caught.

With the coming together of the World Wide Web, pedophiles post secret signs and images on websites and use clandestine wording to alert other pedophiles of their interests. They meet in the Clear Web and exchange ideas. They will then exchange addresses in the Dark Web. We will delve into this in a big way in Chapter Eleven where we talk about child pornography or what is now being called (CAM) Child Abuse Materials. Stay tuned, some of those sites have more than a quarter million pedophiles in them.

To my point about Live.Me, Periscope, and other live streaming sites, it is not the site itself that is the perpetrator. They are simply a vehicle or a facilitator that a pedophile has chosen to use. They have rules and they make it clear it is not to be used for bullying, or illicit sexual behaviors by minors.

As this book is about to go to print I am aware of a Reuters article written by Dave Paresh that identifies technological advancements being used by social media giants. Facebook has announced that they have just removed 8.7 million sexual photos of kids in the last three months. That is encouraging.

Facebook as well as several other apps, have invested in algorithm technologies that identify images that contain both nudity and a child. With the advancement of machine learning tools, technology and social media providers will isolate and remove photos that show minors in a sexualized context. Similar systems also catch users engaged in "grooming" or befriending minors for sexual exploitation. Technology algorithms are not perfect but they are helpful in isolating possible child exploitation on a mass basis.

Facebook's global head of safety, Antigone Davis, told Reuters that "machine (learning tools) helps us prioritize and "more efficiently queue" problematic content for the company's trained team of reviewers". Based on this article, it is clear that mega social media corporations are making some attempt to monitor activity on their sites, even in light of the millions of users posting content on a daily basis.

The truth is, if we hand a device that reaches six billion people to a minor without supervision, who REALLY is responsible for the end result?

It is a tough situation. The site administrators make it clear they believe the site is created for adults and they have zero responsibility if a parent decides to hand a child a smart phone or a tablet. So, the site blames the parent. The parent blames the site saying they should do more to make sure minors cannot be violated on their app. And then everyone calls law enforcement when this goes wrong but the latest technologies are vaporware (poof they are gone, i.e. live streaming) and much of the time law enforcement chastises the minor for sending a naked photo or dancing nude in live streaming. And so, it goes. Thousands of our kids will end up being violated, exploited, blackmailed and some of them will even be sex trafficked while the vicious circle of blame spins round and round.

Let's explore the very tough issue of the role of the minor in online sexual exploitation.

First, I believe that most sex trafficking victims, especially minor sex trafficking victims, had no understanding of where their relationships and choices would lead them. I have yet to meet a sex trafficking victim, minor or adult that understood the impact of the choices they were making and that it would end up with them being violated in the most unspeakable ways over and over.

Because the girl's (or occasionally male's) photos were used in online advertising for commercial sex, we spent much of the last decade educating the public about how sex traffickers operate. Traffickers often took the girl's photos against her will, or after she was drugged, or under dire threat and used them to advertise her online to provide commercial sex services at truck stops, large public events, on the Blade or Track in large cities or at massage parlors etc. The point is that while they may have LOOKED like they were participating willingly, we have spent a decade helping the public and law enforcement understand they are there because of Force, Fraud, Fear or Coercion and most are not acting as free agents.

Up to this place in history, most sex trafficking, sextortion, and social media exploitation victims were singled out by a pedophile or predator and groomed or seduced into a life of exploitation. They typically preyed on foster kids, homeless kids, runaway kids, and pregnant teenagers. These individuals are considered "High Risk" because they had unstable home environments and few financial and emotional support systems which made them available and vulnerable.

Over the past decade we saw an increase in violation of youth that did not fit in the "high risk" category. We would regularly see students who had a 4.0 grade average, who lived in a two-parent household and some even went to private schools. This violation usually happened because the minor hooked up with a stranger on social media without realizing that the new love of their life is really a pimp looking to subtly recruit them into a lifetime of commercial sex and servitude. In some cases, the minor actually met with the predator in person and the result was truly catastrophic often ending in rape.

The hook ups were somewhat random but more likely the connection was made by pimps, pedophiles, and predators who played a game of sending out "bait" by hooking up through instant messaging apps like Snapchat, Kik, Messenger, Instagram, and Twitter. This is the first generation that can talk to strangers by the thousands on a random basis and they do it. Most kids are absolutely positive they can spot a predator so they show little concern about talking with someone they don't know. Of course, when this goes wrong, people like me get involved.

Historically, predators would surf the web seeing who they might "hook up" with and build a trusting relationship. My previous book *"Seduced: The Grooming of America's Teenagers"* outlines in detail all the ways this takes place. Once they built trust then the next stage would be to get the teen to send a provocative or sexual photo or perhaps meet up with them in person. The results were often devastating to the young person AND their families.

BUT WHAT HAPPENS WHEN MINORS PUT THEMSELVES OUT THERE ON THE WORLD WIDE WEB USING PROVOCATIVE AND SALACIOUS BEHAVIOR THAT WILL ATTRACT THE ATTENTION OF SEX BUYERS AND PEDOPHILES?

What I am asking you to consider here are the major changes taking place in the process of finding, grooming, recruiting, and exploitation where the predator no longer is seeking out the victim but rather the VICTIM IS FOR

ALL INTENTS AND PURPOSES TROLLING FOR ATTENTION.

This is a hard discussion. A victim who is sexually violated is still a victim, especially when they are a minor. Looking at live streaming and video chat room sites like Live.Me, Periscope, Omegle, Chatroulette, and others, where is the responsibility? Where is the culpability?

Sex trafficking laws are based on the age of consent (for sex) in that state. In California the age of consent for sex is 18. Whoever wrote that law has not been on a high school campus in California for decades. Sex and sexual overtones are everywhere. More often than not, it is more like sexual "Undertones".

I am often on school campuses and there are many excellent young people trying to be the best they can be and show great maturity and good judgement. I would venture to say even the majority of them.

However, there are also a significant percentage of girls in skin tight tee shirts, shorts showing cheek, and kids filming themselves in very provocative situations. I always come back to the reality that with this generation, many of the kids will excel and use social media responsibly and then there will be a percentage of kids who will ultimately be sexually exploited, some in the worst ways possible. I always wonder, is this a game of chance, of roulette? Or is there some way we can keep them from self-destructing?

This subject is truly the most challenging subject I have ever faced. Most of you that know me personally, know I am a no melodrama, problem solving kind of person. Victims are victims even if they were tricked, lured, coerced, or even somewhat participated willingly without understanding how bad it will get. I don't exaggerate or dramatize. I don't need to as the cases I deal with are already so challenging it is best to stick to understanding how and why this exploitation takes place so we can prevent it from happening to more families and their kids.

What I am witnessing simply makes my heart tremble. As I researched site after site of Live.Me, Periscope, and Omegle, I simply could not get a grasp on how this could be happening. There are many videos of pubescent and prepubescent girls "Twerking" through live streaming where it was "Saved". Many of these very young girls are jiggling their near naked breasts (some don't even have them yet but try anyway) and "Twerk" their butt over and over and then stop to thank people who rewarded them with virtual currency. IT IS A SCAM! Virtual currency has no intrinsic value. You can't really buy anything with it. They are truly, willingly, putting themselves out there in the most cheap and degrading ways, all so they can say they have more virtual currency than anyone else. It gets worse.

I watched a couple of YouTube, Live.Me warnings that had parents talking in them. One was a nine-year-old girl. Get that, NINE. She has not been through puberty. She has zero cognitive adult reasoning skills. This is the generation that was raised on receiving rewards by giving them stickers. One young girl received 20 extra virtual coins for raising her little top. And then they talked her into taking down her bottoms. She said she had no panties on so the viewers gave her extra virtual coins. Keep in mind this is being viewed by hundreds of viewers and she is ever so proud of herself for being so popular.

In a different case I watched another YouTube of parents of warning other parents to be careful with their kids on Live.Me. These parents thought their nine-year-old daughter was on an arts and crafts site. It is still unclear how she could have performed all of these acts without Mom and Dad noticing that dancing, grinding and stripping is not related to arts and crafts but somehow, they did not see it. Before it was discovered their nine-year-old daughter stripped and danced, the broadcast was seen by over 10,000 people.

What no one is really talking about in this case is how many pedophiles may have freeze framed the live streaming into a video and posted it in the Dark Net to be traded, sold and drooled over by thousands of pedophiles FOREVER. I do applaud the parents for being willing to go on the air and warn other parents and teens. Hopefully, when this was done the parents' identity was concealed so the girl will not be further humiliated. These actions will affect both parent and child for a lifetime.

Some of you may be outraged by my next comment, but I feel I must be fair in my analysis. Truthfully, the parents, even though I am certain they are loving and caring parents who would do anything to protect their daughter, participated in this event. When a parent provides a pre-pubescent child with a device that can film them in their most vile acts, they are (most likely without conscious understanding) assisting their child in making child pornography. That is the hard part of this conversation.

If the girl was not stripping, twerking and grinding, they would most likely not be attracting predators and pedophiles. Let me say that a different way. They MAY be attracting pedophiles because they are online and are very young and vulnerable (that is called available and vulnerable) but they will attract a LOT more pedophiles by globally broadcasting a stripping, twerking and grinding performance which is accelerated by receiving attention through virtual currency.

What I conclude is that we are entering an era where the perpetrator no longer will be searching for a victim they can violate but <u>rather will be invited to participate </u>in thousands of live broadcasts where they can interact with a minor seeking attention who has little code of ethics to define what is positive attention. As you project out what the future of this activity is, combined with the realization that future technologies will add bit coin and monetizing capability, it is easy to conclude that the future of minor sex trafficking and social media exploitation is about to explode beyond our wildest expectations.

Stop and think about what I just said. Shortly, per-haps even before this book hits the store shelves, live streaming apps like Live.Me, Periscope, and others will most likely have a money processing protocol. Snapchat has Snap Money now and their slogan is "Now you can monetize a selfie". Just imagine our kids twerking and stripping, grinding and talking to their audiences to encourage them to use "Live-Money" to send them cash. It is not hard to imagine that millions of teens around the world will be starring in homemade live streaming porn performances to get a new set of Nikes or pay their tuition or just to brag about how much they made last night.

The really critical issue here is how are we, as a society and law enforcement, to deal with this? Can we really pretend she does not know what she is doing? If we admit that she is only nine and has the sexual and intellectual capacity of a nine-year-old, then why is much of the advanced society providing free access to the global internet for nine, ten, eleven, twelve-year-old kids that have no adult capacity in decision making?

Additionally, they have little understanding of what sex is at nine. There is no doubt in my mind however, that these activities will form this child's perception of sexual relationships far before she starts through puberty. More important, that sexual self-image will not be based on her value and worth as a chosen child of God who experiences sex as a joyful and respectful give and take between two mature individuals who cherish and protect each other.

I seriously doubt that this little girl has a solid understanding of why people are cheering her on. And I doubt that a nine-year-old understands pedophilia, fetishes, the Dark Net and child pornography issues enough to realize that she is not all that popular but rather a commodity to be drooled over, traded, sold and exploited repeatedly. Having said that, if we as a society realize that a nine-year-old does not have the mental capacity to understand what is really taking place here, why on earth are parents providing her with the resources so she can make that happen?

It is a fascinating deal to me. We don't give nine-year-old's keys to the car. We don't even give16-year-old keys to the car without an education of the potential consequences if the privilege is abused. We say the age for drinking is at least 16 or 18 in most states because we recognize that young people do not have the adult reasoning to make informed and educated choices until they are well past puberty. And yet there is almost NO education about how predators misuse the Internet before we hand a phone to very young children.

The challenge in writing a book like "Societal Shift" is that crimes are coming in daily. It is like a technology criminal super highway. It is nearly impossible to keep up. The work of Million Kids is to research these cases and understand the impact of technological advances and how it will affect us as a society. Even working seventy hours a week with a full support team, it is a significant challenge to filter out excess "noise" of technologies that make our lives exciting or uncomfortable and discern which cases are the most important to relate to the public.

As I am writing about the app Live.Me, I see a headline "Paedophile (Pedophile is spelled Paedophile in the UK) becomes the first to be convicted of using Live.Me streaming app to incite girls into sexual activity." This is an article by Rachel Roberts of the Independent Online from the UK.

The article is about the conviction of Glen Friend, 18, a convicted pedophile who seduced a nine-year-old girl to expose herself on Live.Me. He was jailed for additional years and was the first case in the UK involving Live.Me. The article states, "users have little control over who views their posts". So, I ask you, "IF A PARENT KNOWS THIS (and I suspect they don't), WHY WOULD A PARENT ALLOW A NINE-YEAR-OLD TO BE ON LIVE.ME?"

In this case, Glen Friend had just left prison having served a sentence for breaching sex offender notification requirements. Let me make this clear. Glen Friend is not only convicted of a prior sexual offense, he is in prison for breaching the terms of the sentence for a prior sexual offense. So, it is fair to say, this guy is a fierce and committed sexual predator. To my point in the "Societal Shift", it is a world without borders for cartels, organized crime, predators and YES CONVICTED SEX OFFENDERS, who can access, groom, recruit and exploit our young people.

In another report by the Daily Mail on the case of Glen Friend, there is an indication that he coerced the nine-year-old girl to expose herself and then posted the video online as part of a game of dare. That particular video was viewed by almost 300 users including a group of ten pedophiles whom police are still trying to trace. The article suggests that Friend had been using Live.Me to contact young children and he had 355 followers on the site, some of whom are suspected pedophiles.

While most of us read articles like this and recoil in horror, I try to put myself in the position of the victim, the pedophile, and law enforcement to see what we can learn.

First, we see that Glen Friend KNOWS that there are plenty of kids on Live.Me and apparently so do all his pedophile friends because they are trolling there.

Secondly, you can assume (or at least parents and law enforcement SHOULD) that ANY illicit photo of a child or teen they can get their hands on will be traded, sold, shared by pedophiles in child pornography rings both in the Clear Web and the Dark Net. It will be passed around forever. So maybe there is a lesson that when Live.Me says they have an age restriction, it should be heeded.

Equally important is the lesson we can learn as we examine the victim in this situation. She is NINE. She knows how to access strangers on Live.Me. She is easy prey. She wants to get attention. She wants reinforcement (from a stranger) that she is attractive, acceptable, etc. She is willing to expose herself as part of a dare. She KNOWS how to not only make a video on Live.Me but she also knows how to upload it online without the help of an adult. Do her parents understand her immaturity and vulnerability and just choose to look the other way? Is it possible that the parents are not involved with her life enough to know that their daughter is a dare seeker, who will aggressively seek out strangers on the Internet and do what it takes to please them?

OK, I get it. I am being VERY hard on a nine-year-old. What I want you, the reader, to think about is that if a parent is handing a child a device that will make their child available to the whole world, there should be substantial thought about the level of that child's maturity, decision making skills, tendencies to seek attention, willingness to take chances, and if their child has the skills to make and upload a video that can be posted online.

Speaking of dares, perhaps this book will open the eyes of parents around the globe to understand that when their child goes online, they are thrusting their child smack dab into a world of adult men and women, many of whom are pedophiles. Parents, are you believing in your heart of hearts that your child is ready, willing and mature enough to stand against hundreds of very slick child molesters who will pull every trick in the book to access and violate your child? IS YOUR CHILD REALLY READY TO STAND AGAINST THAT?

I find these articles quite interesting. It makes it clear that total strangers can access our kids and provide them with "likes" and "electronic gifts" from other users. But in the article where the nine-year-old girl received over 10,000 views it indicates that the parents blame the App producer. "The Owners of this app seriously needs to do something about their security". You may think I am hardcore and narrow minded, but the APP OWNERS make it clear that minors should not be on their app. The app owners did not put a nine-year-old on their app. THE PARENTS DID.

I am grateful that this situation was found by the parents, law enforcement responded, and a prosecution ended with a prison sentence for an experienced pedophile. Hopefully there will be millions more as the App owner recognizes the dangers and begins to try to develop a way to force the public to make decisions that will protect their children.

There are many good uses for the Live.Me technology. **I applaud Live.Me for trying to form a global monitoring program.** But as they reach the stage of having a BILLION users at some point, the bottom line is that Live.Me must invest in billions of dollars of advertising to educate parents about the VALUE of their software and the DANGERS so that parents begin to take age restrictions on usage seriously. The question is how to get parents to stop, listen, and take these restrictions on technology to heart?

In a few short months Live.Me will be old and antiquated technology. There will be a new and shiny, whiz bang technology that provides even more unlimited access to our children with even more relationship building incentives. As I have said over and over, it will be a "World without Borders and a Home without Walls." The sooner our society recognizes this fact, the less children will be violated.

What is really scary is that lately we are seeing parents hand very small children their phones to entertain them. Playing on the phone will be perceived as an entitlement by the time they are seven or eight years old. The craziness here is that once you hand a three-year-old a phone to play with, just try getting it away from them. You might need a body guard because I assure you, you are about to witness a temper tantrum that will attract a small crowd.

What about the Parents? Most parents are good, concerned, and caring parents but they feel impotent on the subject of understanding technology advances. Most parents will tell you that they TRY to stay current, but it is just happening too fast. Most parents will provide a child with a cell phone along with a lecture "You be careful on that thing, you hear?" And then they hope their child listens. But "HOPE "is not a strategy.

It is difficult to have an honest discussion on this subject without suggesting that parents need to have a responsibility in this issue. Truthfully, very few kids would have a phone if the parents were not making them available. It is seen as an entitlement. Everyone else has one. And the parent does not want their child to be a nerd. I totally get it.

Certainly, the major carriers (Sprint, AT&T, T-Mobile) get it as they all have family plans to ensure that everyone has access to a phone in case of emergency. Funny, does anyone remember how we ever handled emergencies in1985 before iPhones?

Certainly, we don't want our kids to live in a bubble. They need to function in real life and find a way to fit into society as a functioning and responsible participant. As technology accelerates, the thought of having a young person without a phone will feel like living in the time of the Flintstones.

Some kids are more responsible, more mature, and show more sound judgement than others. It really does not seem to have to do with grade average, affluency of the family, or even their social skills. Sometimes I think the kids in well to do families are even more vulnerable. It is often those kids that have the latest and greatest gadgets. It makes me shudder to think of the number of kids I have met in private high schools that have a Dark Net account because Mom and Dad are not home often and they have the financial resources to have the latest technology.

I have tried relentlessly to understand what makes the difference in cases where a child or teen becomes a victim of sextortion, social media exploitation or sex trafficking. We know pedophiles are looking for available and vulnerable. But what about lonely? What about insecurity? What about poor boundaries, or risk-taking tendencies, or just poor judgement?

To me there are several critical factors in parenting that can make the difference. The most important factor I believe is helping children understand their importance in the family unit. Truthfully, the family is quickly becoming a thing of the past. Even when together, families (including Mom and Dad) spend all their time on the phone. The long-term effect of this is to erode the parent's implied value in the child's mind.

A young person who lives in a cyber world is being bombarded with all kinds of ideas, values, and perceived risk levels that are separate and apart from the values of the parent. That is why it is so easy for a total stranger to get a nine-year-old (or a 14-year-old) to strip naked and dance for virtual currency. In the back of their minds they know if they get caught, Mom or Dad will "kill them" (figure of speech). Interesting, even though they KNOW it is being broadcast out on the World Wide Web potentially to thousands, they somehow believe that Mom and Dad will never know about it. And for most parents, it is a fairly sure bet that they won't see it. Or in the one case of the

Live.Me event, they did not see it until 10,000 other people had seen it.

I also think it is important for both parents to have a MUTUALLY agreed on strategy. There should be no daylight between the parents on the strategy. If one parent is positioned as too strict or the other parent is more liberal with privileges so they are the favorite parent, the child is the loser: Every time. No exceptions. What is important here is that there is a DECISION made by the family when and under what conditions a minor can have a phone or computer access and under what circumstances.

It should be an agreement between parent and teen. Hopefully, the parents are informed and can share with the teen what an amazing opportunity and privilege it is to have a phone. But there are rules. It is put away during dinner. It does not go to bed with you. And you and the young person will regularly go through the phone together.

I also think it is important for the parents and teen to look at a phone as a family partnership. The parents are paying for it, but they believe their child is seriously going to be a leader and an example for their younger brothers and sisters. The discussion should include an agreement that the parent expects their child or teen to share with them before they install ANY apps they have not previously agreed on. And the discussion should include all the ways that a predator might use that app inappropriately to cause harm.

It is absolutely critical that a parent check a young person's phone regularly. Truthfully, it is the parents' phone as they are paying the bill and it is in fact a "Family" phone. As you have already read in this book, a child who is dancing and twerking provocatively can be viewed by over 10,000 people in a very short period of time. And those photos have GPS attached to them unless the parent has disabled the GPS. So, the child's life and the life of the entire family are up for grabs if a parent is not paying close attention.

It is also important that if a minor has an app, the entire family needs to understand how that app works. Talk together on how it can be used inappropriately. It might be helpful for Mom and Dad (and teens) to follow Million Kids on Facebook as we post new cases of exploitation several times a day and that would help the entire family understand how pimps, predators and pedophiles are using specific apps to exploit young people.

You may think you really don't want to traumatize your children, and I agree. But if you don't educate your child, then they are a sitting duck to be violated. As I have said repeatedly, if you hand a child a smart phone or tablet before you have "The Sex Talk", I guarantee you someone else will be educating your child on sexual behaviors that you may find horrifying.

As I began to understand the far-reaching implications of this technology, I realized that it has the potential to be a sort of interactive, live version of a Backpage Ad. For those of you that have little knowledge of sex trafficking, Backpage was the most infamous website that pimps and perpetrators used to advertise photos of the sex trafficking victims they were selling. While there were many sites, probably hundreds of sites that offered escort and sex services for sale, Backpage and Craig's List were the most famous. The pimp or bottom girl would take promiscuous photos of the victim and pay money to place an ad on the website. Most recently the ads appeared under "Women Dating Men" which of course was a total misnomer. Most of the ads were of scantily clad women in provocative positions and many had no heads or facial photos. No one in their right mind ever thought they were looking to go out for a quiet evening of dinner and intellectual conversation.

In 2018 the owners of Backpage were arrested and the site was taken down. Almost simultaneously the federal legislators passed FOSTA (Fight Online Sex Trafficking Act) and it was signed by President Trump. Among the many provisions were statements that anyone who is (or was) advertised on a sex services website could sue the owner of the website for damages if they could prove they were subsequently sexually or physically exploited as a result of that advertisement.

This combination of events got the attention of the commercial sex industry and they began to scatter like rats. Very quickly we began to see sleazy, small time websites pop up advertising local talent. It was obvious these were low rent website owners who had no assets and therefore were not afraid of being sued. We saw the large-scale website owners close down in the U.S and set up their websites offshore where a victim or law enforcement would have trouble executing a U.S. lawsuit. Now the victim is being even more violated. Without U.S. restrictions on publishing, many of the photos and offers for services are extremely damaging to the victim while simultaneously being distributed worldwide as hard-core pornography. The victim has little recourse and will most likely never be able to get the photos off the Internet.

Of greater concern to me, is the way live streaming technologies will become the interactive connection between victim and sex buyer without the ease of having a one stop shop like Backpage. Until recently, Law Enforcement could see all the victims being advertised on one site (Backpage) and set up reverse stings to find them and free them. With the onset of live streaming services that attract thousands of viewers and the closing of Backpage, it will be more difficult for law enforcement to see the individual sites where victims are being advertised online.

Think about how live streaming works now. The girl goes "live" and starts doing a provocative dance. Millions of viewers are alerted and begin to follow her. They give her virtual currency (emojis or virtual stickers) indicating their approval and suggesting particular fetishes they would like to see advanced.

It is a single site amongst millions of other sites and will be hard to locate by law enforcement.

Once a perspective customer is connected to the performer, she can then direct them to her private website or even a hidden website in the Dark Net that requires a particular address. She can easily accept pre-payments through Snap Cash, Facebook Money, Messenger, or Bitcoin. She can even set them up for a monthly subscription to her ongoing library of nude and erotic videos. As I am writing this, I see a link on YouTube of a young woman bragging that she made $10,000 on Live.Me. She also instructs others how to do this.

These technologies will forever change commercial sex. Unfortunately, it will also make combating child sex trafficking much harder for law enforcement and prosecutors.

Having said all of the above, I want to make it very clear that it is NOT the technology that is causing exploitation of our children. There are many legitimate and good uses for Live.Me live streaming. I may even consider using the technology myself to further educate the public about how all of this works. There are thousands of people on live streaming apps like

Periscope and Live.Me that are using it in a constructive and engaging manner. Some are selling real estate; some are teaching cooking or sewing or painting; some are teaching foreign languages or school curriculums; some are giving motivational programs. The technology itself is fantastic.

Creative and entrepreneurial individuals will have a whole new world opened to them to share their talents and expertise. Sites like Live.Me will provide a professional vehicle for them to become known across the nation or even around the globe. They will be able to charge for their expertise. The potential for using technology for good is both exciting and motivating. We are truly about to open our "home without walls" to global market places, have access to more knowledge, and exposure to unique and inspiring goods we can only imagine today.

To their credit, Live.Me is even encouraging individuals to become monitors of their services to watch for the misuse of their technology and report it! GOOD FOR THEM! Assuming they continue and expand this opportunity, it might help solve some of the "Great Conundrum".

The parent buys a "Child" a phone and the "Child" goes on an app and misuses the technology. They end up being exploited. The parent blames the app, the app blames the parent, and in the meantime the child's life (and the life of her family) is changed for- ever. WHO IS RESPONSIBLE?

However, I feel Live.Me's approach to engaging the public to help monitor illegal and illicit use of their technology might be a start in the right direction. As six billion people come on board the World Wide Web, this is going to be one of the greatest chal- lenges of all time.

This is one of the reasons Million Kids exists. For nearly ten years, Susie Carpenter, the Media and Marketing Director for Million Kids has posted cases of social media exploitation several times a day on Facebook: Million Kids. We realized early on that parents, teachers, law enforcement, civic leaders and teenagers need to see the cases of how pedo- philes and predators misuse technology in a way that exploits our kids.

While sometimes it is hard to read these cases, we feel that it is critical to understand the various new apps and how pedophiles employ them for exploitation. Very few organizations are doing this research and communicating the updates on a daily basis.

This work is hard work and it takes money and financial investments to keep it going and expand it across the nation quickly. We appreciate everyone who donates to Million Kids and helps support our work so we can very quickly communicate each new trend and technology advancement and how it will both benefit us but more important, how it could be used by a pedophile, predator, gang member or cartel to harm a child.

THANK YOU FOR YOUR SUPPORT.

CHAPTER THREE:

THE PSYCHOLOGICAL IMPACT OF SOCIAL MEDIA

First let's take a look at the impact social media has on our relationships.

Psychologists tell us that when ALL individuals (adults, teens and yes KIDS) use social media, it is processed as a harmless and risk-free activity. When using a smart phone or chatting in a chat room, most of us tend to deny our normal instincts and we overcome our inhibitions. We simply do and say things we would normally never do.

For instance, imagine a 14-year-old girl going to the mall and meeting, for the first time, a 28-year-old guy and after an hour of talking they meet in the mall bathroom and strip naked, take a photo and hand it to each other. It is just simply NOT going to happen. We have inhibitions. Most of us have a moral barometer that says, not only is this dangerous, it is downright icky!

However, that same girl, with the right grooming and flirting, can often be talked into taking a perceived harmless selfie and sending it off to a total stranger who has seduced her. This is only possible because the Internet gives us a distorted sense of reality. It gives us a perceived notion that the Internet is something of a game where there is no reality, no real-life consequences for our decisions.

Time and again we see behavior on the Internet that would be hard to fathom in real life.

Recently, I saw an interview on Fox News with Sean Parker, one of the original developers of Facebook. He mentioned that Facebook was designed as a "SOCIAL VALIDATION FEEDBACK LOOP". WOW is that powerful. Think about what he is saying. We all want approval. Certainly, there is nothing new or unique about that. It is an innate desire.

Facebook led the revolution for instant gratification and gave the users the ability to feed the public, maybe even bait people, and receive the approval they crave. It must work because today they are a trillion-dollar company.

Think about this. In previous generations, public approval was something that was earned. A person was recognized based on their accomplishments and contributions to society. There were not a lot of accolades, but they were meaningful. You got up every day and went to work and occasionally your wife or mother or the neighbors would give you a compliment. As an adult you really were expected to be self-sustaining and approval was something that was the icing on the cake.

Today, approval comes through posting the latest photo of your kitty chasing a bird and you wait to see how many "likes" you get so you can gauge if your popularity is still intact. That is what Sean Parker meant by social validation feedback loop. It is nearly instantaneous and it gives you a statistical gauge to evaluate if you are popular or not and if people care about you.

The challenge is that we are raising a generation of kids who look to OUTSIDERS to feel good about themselves. We are opening the door to social media platforms where the satisfaction for the craving for approval comes from complete strangers.

What gets all of us, adults and teens alike, is our sense of invincibility. That is especially true of pre-pubescent kids who have little understanding of how evil some evil can get. We approach most decisions in our lives believing that evil will not happen to us. And that is right and fair. We cannot live our lives dominated by fear; Nor should we. We do not want our young people to live under a cloud of fear and intimidation.

From a very young age we take our children by the hand and teach them to look both ways before crossing the street. (Well, except in the Costco parking lot. I swear grown adults lead little kids behind moving cars in most Costco parking lots teaching them that they have the right away against a three-ton car- ugh. (I digress. I could not help myself. It is a personal beef of mine).

For the most part, we teach kids how to cross busy streets. We do not require that they live their lives on a curb because the street is too busy to cross. We TEACH them how to cross the street. And if they don't listen, there are consequences.

The Internet is no different. There is a wonderful world waiting for them, tremendous education and networking opportunities assuming they choose the safe and quality path.

The challenge to THIS generation is that most parents have not crossed most of the streets in the world of Internet. They have little experience with apps, chat rooms, and even less with avatars and online gaming chat rooms. Very few parents I know play the games they buy for their children and teens. They don't sit with them and see what is being fed into their child's mind. They don't listen in on the chat rooms. They either have no idea of the dangers lurking beyond the positive applications or if they do recognize imminent danger, their primary strategy is prayer, threats, resignation, and an unspoken belief that they can play the "odds" and that their child is brilliant and won't get sucked in. THAT IS NOT AN EFFECTIVE STRATEGY.

The Internet feels like this place where we can try out all kinds of bizarre and illogical behavior. If you don't believe this is true, just go to YouTube, type in "Omegle" and brace yourself. You may want to turn the sound down as it is a cesspool of filthy language. Omegle is an old app, mostly out of style now but in its heyday, kids went crazy on it. Omegle was one of the first video chat rooms where kids could sit in their bedrooms and meet complete strangers while Mom was at the grocery store. Still, to this day, we will see an occasional case where a teen met up with someone from Omegle and ended up being violated.

What is very disconcerting is how young many of these kids are that are featured in the YouTube videos that are recorded from Omegle. You are supposed to be an adult to be on Omegle which is somewhat humorous because an adult (well at least MOST adults) would find this activity very juvenile. Minors are not supposed to be allowed on Omegle but some adult has provided them with access and left them unsupervised. In one video I used to show at my presentations there was a 15-year-old guy pretending to hang himself and it was witnessed by what looked like an 8-year-old boy and 10 or 11-year-old girls.

Omegle's logo is "Talk with Strangers". I am not making this up. The idea is that you sign on and a total stranger will randomly be assigned to your chat room. You have no idea who it is going to be and what they are going to look like. It is truly stranger roulette. It is not an occasional stranger encounter sandwiched in with people you know, it is every encounter. It is the purpose of the app to meet up with strangers. That is why it is the perfect playground for pedophiles.

I feel that a psychological examination of behaviors on Omegle is an important lesson for parents to consider. First of all most adults would not be on Omegle. It is a waste of time and simply too bizarre. If an adult is on Omegle, they are most likely looking to hook up with a minor. But what I hope you will take the time to consider is this. The behaviors you see on Omegle's YouTube videos are behaviors you would most likely NOT see in real life in a group setting or an environment where one thousand people would be watching. On Omegle, kids and adults dress up in scary costumes, some look like the devil, some pretend to hang themselves, some film themselves going to the bathroom (seriously), others do weird sex acts.

Omegle is just one of many sites that allows our teens to meet total strangers and role play publicly while sitting in their own bedroom. The videos are then posted on YouTube and monitored for the number of hits which reinforces their popularity and acceptance by others. The great concern is not only that the child is being exposed to very bizarre and sometimes degrading behavior, filthy language and questionable people, but that minors are posting their encounters to seek approval. Very few Omegle videos posted on YouTube are a public image that most parents would be proud of.

Hope is not a protection plan.

What we are seeing are parents all over the world, playing the odds their child will not become a victim. As soon as a child is violated, and the parents discover it, they are in a real crisis. I have had parent after parent tell me, that the signs were there, but they simply could not allow themselves to look further. The parent wants to believe this is not as bad as it is or that their child will be the exception. And they assuage the fear and the guilt with the thinking that everyone does it, so their child will be safe. Nothing could be further from the truth.

While writing this book, I see a case headline posted by Sarah Perez of Tech Crunch. "Roblox responds to the hack that allowed a child's avatar to be raped in its game". This is just one of thousands of cases that come across my desk each year involving many different apps and games. This type of potential exploitation is not unique to Roblox as it is happening all the time.

In this case a 7-year-old girl was playing on Roblox, a hugely popular online game for kids and it was hacked in such a way that two male avatars began to gang rape the 7-year-old's avatar on the virtual playground. Fortunately, Mom was nearby and the girl was informed enough to realize that something was not right and she showed it to her mother who wisely, immediately shut it off.

In this article the mother stated: "At first, I couldn't believe what I was seeing. My sweet and innocent daughter's avatar was being violently gang raped on a playground by two males. A female observer approached them and proceeded to jump on her body at the end of the act. Then the three characters ran away, leaving my daughter's avatar laying on her face in the middle of the playground. I cannot describe the shock, disgust and guilt that I am feeling right now."

Certainly, we applaud the mother for training her daughter to report and being nearby when her daughter was online. But still, I contend that if you are going to put a very young child on the Internet open to the public, there will always be a chance that they will be exposed to many things you, as a parent may not agree with. There is a reason it is called, "The World Wide Web."

I understand that some of you may judge me to be rabid on this subject but I have seen way too many of these cases where things go wrong. For a parent to allow a 9-year-old child in a public video chat room, is the equivalent of taking your beautiful 9-year-old daughter down to the local bus depot or bar and dropping her off for the afternoon. Parents seem to want to deny the fact that many of the people in these chat rooms, you would not invite into your own living room. And yet they blindly, naively, hoping against hope allow their prepubescent kid to take their chances, believing that their child will be the exception to being violated.

The parent has not understood the concepts involved in social media and living in a fantasy world where a child believes they can experiment and there will be no consequences for their real-life decisions. In fact, I would argue that a 9, 10, 11-year-old kid does not have enough cognitive reasoning development in their sweet little brains to even be able to project out what the consequence COULD be. As fine a child as they probably are, they simply do not yet have the hardware for critical thinking.

As we are about to look at the "Psychology of Grooming" in the next chapter I would like to relate a story about a case I had a couple of years back that illustrates both the grooming process and the challenges for a young person (and sometimes adults) to grasp the concept that living in the fantasy world of social media can have real life consequences.

This is a case involving a hard-working single mother trying to raise a 15-year-old responsible daughter without a male role model in her life. The Mom was a great Mom, but she had to work in order to be able to pay the rent. The father had long since abandoned them both emotionally and financially. The daughter was a typical 15-year-old with normal school activities and an occasional rebellious attitude but nothing serious. Every day while Mom was at work this girl played X Box. She developed a crush on a guy from Australia who was in her chat room. They talked every day and because of playing the game together she was very loyal to him. Since he lived in a different country neither Mom or daughter thought there was any risk in the relationship.

Looking back at this case now, I realize that this girl was trying to fill the hole in her heart because she had been abandoned by her father. And she was probably lonely because she spent a lot of time by herself. These factors would make her "Available and Vulnerable", which is the primary criteria for a pedophile or predator.

One day after several months of playing X Box together the guy said, "Hey, I want to send you a gift. What is your address?". Think about this scenario. In real life this girl probably would not give her address to a total stranger because it is dangerous. But social media and online gaming chat rooms build fantasy relationships where most minors and some adults cannot "experience" the perceived threat.

Without a moment's hesitation, the girl gave her address. After all he is in Australia. How dangerous can it be? Immediately after receiving the address, the fellow gamer said "Hey, I just realized that my Aunt from Australia is on vacation in San Diego and I think she is on her way to Las Vegas (which is exactly passing through this girl's home town).

He asked if the Aunt could stop by and meet her and give her a little gift from him. Without thinking it out, the girl agreed to it.

Fortunately for all involved, the next morning as Mom was going out the door to work, the girl realized that people she had never met were about to come by their home and meet her when no one was with her. THIS IS A CRITICAL POINT. Think about this. In Cyberspace the girl was quickly seduced to provide her personal address and did not experience it as a danger. And she did not mention it to her Mom.

Fortunately, in real life, the girl almost immediately realized that she had put herself in danger. In real life, she overcame her embarrassment and reached out to her MOM. As Mom was going out the door, she suddenly said, "Hey Mom, my friend's Aunt from Australia is coming by in about half hour to give me a gift. Will you stay home with me so I won't be alone when they get here?". PRAISE GOD she overcame the cyber fantasy and realized she had put herself in danger. Many young people do not or they are so embarrassed they don't tell anyone until it is too late.

After Mom overcame her initial rage/fear-based reaction, she quickly called in to work to say she would be late and they devised a plan for Mom to wait on the curb for the guests and the girl would stay in the house until Mom could assess the situation. Sure enough, a white van with dark windows showed up and there was an older man, a younger man and a woman. Mom said the younger man scared her to death. They had a cheap box of candy and they wanted to meet the daughter. The mother told them the daughter had gone on to school.

While the girl was hiding in the house, she texted her friend in Australia to say that the Aunt was there. When she did, the text went to the young man standing in front of her Mom at the curb. THERE NEVER WAS A MAN IN AUSTRALIA. Whoever the girl had been talking to lived somewhere in Southern California. The weeks of chat room fantasy was simply a grooming tool to manipulate the girl and build trust so she would reveal her address. My guess, based on years of these kinds of cases, is that had the Mom not stayed home and intervened, this girl would have been grabbed, forced into the van, broken, drugged and put into hard core prostitution. This would have been a case of "Sex Trafficking".

But it all started with a fantasy relationship. It was based on the belief that somewhere out there is a guy/man who thought she was the greatest thing since sliced bread. We all want that. It is normal. Predators understand that. And they understand the power of social media in helping a person create an environment where all their dreams come true. Even if we are suspicious that it is too good to be true, We ALL want to believe. Predators are counting on that.

CHAPTER FOUR:

THE PSYCHOLOGY OF GROOMING- FANTASY RELATIONSHIPS

Fantasy is a powerful motivator. It gets people to do things they otherwise would not do.

When I wrote my first book *"Seduced: The Grooming of America's Teenagers"* I wrote an entire chapter on fantasy relationships. With several years of experience of researching cases and sitting with families and hearing victims of trafficking, sextortion and social media exploitation, I now realize that I was just pulling back the layers of a very complex situation.

It really is a fascinating concept. Many of you that read *"Seduced"* may recall the situation where the young man at Pomona High School made me mad. The situation involved the online video game: Grand Theft Auto". GTA-V was one of the biggest video game successes in the world. Certainly, a player was not obligated, but if he CHOSE to, a player could invest $20, $50 or $70 using his Bitcoin account to have sex with the virtual prostitute and then kill her to get (most) of his money back. I was stunned to see how many minors (kids under 18) who are either aware of it or who had used their Bitcoins to participate in the virtual sex act and subsequent virtual murder.

The way GTA-V works (just like thousands of others), is that once you pay to have sex with the prostitute and you kill her, your score goes up and you can get most of your money back. I was giving a presentation at a local high school to about 450 students and asked them how many of them had GTA-V or had played it. About 375 of them raised their hands. Then I asked the 375 students how many had had virtual sex with the prostitute in the game. About 300 students raised their hands. Then I asked how many of the 300 killed the prostitute to get their money back. About 200 students had killed the prostitute. Then I asked the 200 students how many felt bad about killing the prostitute in the game. The answer – TWO.

What sent me down the path to understanding the phenomenon of "numbness to danger in a virtual world" was the conversations I had with hundreds of teenage online game players using MMORPG's (massive-multi-player-online-role-playing games). When we asked them about virtual sex within a video game, most seemed oblivious. Almost NONE of the teens I asked perceived that sex was being used as a weapon. I asked the teens if they felt bad about killing the prostitute and 90% of them replied, "No. It is no big deal. It is just a game."

During a training event with delinquent teens at a local police department, I asked several boys if they "killed the cop" in GTA-V. One young man laughed and said, "Yeah, he backed up twice, but I "Got him". I pointed out that he was in a Police Station and there were two officers next to him, he simply said "Yeah, but it is JUST A GAME!"

Have you ever stopped to dissect the TRUTH of this act? We are teaching kids that to increase their score and gain the acceptance of others, it is OK to use virtual sex to satisfy yourself and impress others. It is in fact "sex as a weapon". It also dehumanizes sex. Most kids will tell you sex in these video games is not really sex. But if it is NOT really sex, why would you pay $50.00 for it?

To my knowledge there are no research projects currently being conducted to determine if young people are pleasuring themselves during this event or simply participating as a third-party viewer when they engage with virtual sex with the prostitute inside the game. Some of you may find this line of thinking offensive, but I believe it is extremely relevant to understand the interaction of fantasy with real life actions as it relates to online gaming chat rooms and real-life pedophile grooming, isolation, and exploitation.

I bring up this very sensitive matter because it will make all the difference in the world in understanding the grooming process. GTA-V by its very design operates in public chat rooms where you engage in dialogue with others. If hormonal early pubescent players are purchasing virtual sex from a prostitute under the guise of getting their scores up, and they are emotionally engaging in the virtual sex act, then they will be INFINITELY more likely to engage in conversation about sex to those members of the chat room. I contend they will be a million more times likely to become victims recruited by a predator because they see a mutual acceptance. It may even be perceived as an intimate exchange with someone in the chat room they are loyal to.

While we are on the subject, I really would like to explore with you about the desensitizing of the sexual relationship in the age of social media. Time and again, teens tell me that the "Sex" they pay for on the Internet in video games is not "Sex". What is concerning to me is that there are virtually no resources to say what sex is or what sex SHOULD be on the Internet and in real life.

We have a generation of young people who are hormonal and are seeking to be loved and approved of by another and we hand them a device that can reach the entire world. There are few discussions about what makes a healthy, empowering relationship and what is an exploitative relationship. We literally turn the kids loose to roam the earth to see what they can find (or what finds them) with very little instruction or guidance as to what they are looking for or even more important how to evaluate what they find or what finds them.

Think about social media and sex. It is blatant, one-sided, negotiable, and everywhere. It is 9-year-olds twerking;15-year-olds making money live streaming their bare anatomy; it is anal sex as virgins; and in most of social media, it is one-sided where sex is used as a weapon to make sure your team wins in video games.

Of course, nothing could be further from the truth in real life. What these folks are really seeking is real life, honest, intimate relationships. They are looking for interaction where someone actually cares for them as a human being, respects them, and enjoys their full personality including intellect, integrity, humor and yes, physical appearance in the context of a respectful and responsible relationship.

It will be interesting to see the long-term effect on our society as we raise a generation of youth who use sex as a weapon in an online video game while still trying to navigate a REAL relationship in REAL life that requires intimacy, vulnerability, and respect for each other. One cannot help but wonder what kind of real-life implications we are building with a generation that is exposed to adult porn in video gaming connected to a score where sex is a weapon. We all hope and pray they will grow up to be mature, holy, moral human beings that can build a strong adult sexual relationship. Only time with tell.

Most kids want you to believe that they can live in the fantasy world, making decisions that will increase their score and gain the approval of their chat room buddies but that their actions will have no real-life consequences. My experience in dealing with sextortion and sex trafficking victims is quite different. I believe that once you are living in the world of tweets, texts, and flirts in stranger hookups or teen online dating sites, it may seem like a FANTASY with no danger. However, the minute you meet up with your new-found friend or send them a nude or partially nude photo, your life will change forever, and so will the world of your family.

Looking back on all the situations where I have been involved with a case of trafficking or sextortion, I realize now that this line of thinking really only touches the surface of the impact of fantasy relation-ships and being groomed by a predator.

In my work, I have witnessed that some of the very best kids end up being violated.

In one local case, there was a 14-year-old girl with a two-parent household. Mom and Dad were strapped for cash but they wanted their child not to be different than the other kids at school. They worked over time and bought their daughter a smart phone. Neither Mom nor Dad knew anything about technology, so they simply bought, lectured on safety and prayed for the best.

One day this girl's behavior changed. They began to argue with her. Then one day this beautiful 14-year-old girl got in a fight with her Mom and Dad. They took her to school where she went in one door and out the other. She snuck off to the local mall and met her new found love. (I have seen this scenario play out hundreds of times in my

work). The new boyfriend was actually a pimp in South Central Los Angeles. He took her to LA and for nearly nine weeks this girl was traded back and forth among the gangs of LA. It is a true tragedy. Her life and the life of her family are forever scarred.

Million Kids often assists parents in looking for missing kids. We assisted in this case. I will never forget the anguish of the girl's father. One day he said to me. "In the back seat of my car, in my own living room, I stood by as another man came into my life and stole my precious daughter. I knew nothing about computers and I had no way of understanding what was happening."

First, this is not a bad Dad. To the contrary, he is an excellent man who cared deeply about his daughter. However, when families provide communication equipment that will access the entire world and not prepare themselves with the reality of the capability for predators to access their children, it is destined to be a disaster.

MORAL BAROMETER – DANGER DETECTOR

There is also a really unique factor for minors in dealing with social media and technology. It is a sense of invincibility. Just like the parents choose not to look at the potential for predators to violate their child, minors themselves have no moral barometer and no danger detector to realize when they are in danger. Again, this is based on the reality that in the Internet world, it all FEELS like a fantasy. The perception is there are no consequences.

Let's look at the case of the Musical.ly app. Certainly the app itself is a fine app with some of the best intentions. The app, in essence, is a community where talented individuals come together, record a short video of their singing, dancing, playing an instrument, etc. It is the equivalent of an online community similar to the TV show "America's Got Talent". It is a way for talent to rise to the top and get noticed by millions of people through social media.

According to Biz Carson, a Senior Tech Reporter with Business Insider, "the DIY music video app first came on the scene in 2014, but exploded to the top of the App Store very quickly swapping top places in the App Store with Snapchat and Instagram."

"The 15 second videos are......a mix of teenage boys thumping their chests to a song, to gymnastics routines set to music to acting out funny lyrics from songs." "Today more than 10 million people use the app daily and more than 70 million people are registered users."

In order to be discovered, the app suggests that you need lots of followers. Most teens have no more than 100 followers so the app suggests that if you want to be the next Katy Perry, then you must have thousands of followers to be discovered. The app also suggests a program where you can get 75,000 new followers so you can be discovered. That sounds pretty exciting, thinking that your daughter could be a star and be discovered.

Think about this. Remember vulnerable and available are the primary criteria for predators to be able to access, groom, and recruit young people. Just consider the mathematical odds of a child being accessed by a predator in this scenario.

Let's say they are able to use the program to reach 75,000 followers. The child is going to be excited and think they are about to be famous. But…What if 1% of those followers are pedophiles preying on the hopes and dreams of a young guy or girl? That is 750 Pedophiles. And that child is seeking their approval. Imagine taking your 12-year-old precious daughter by the hand and leading her through a room of over 750 pedophiles where she is seeking their approval. I assure you based on the work that I do, that at least

10% of those 750 pedophiles will pose as sexy young teen boys who want to be her boyfriend. Even worse, some will pose as successful talent agents that will guarantee her a contract – available and vulnerable.

The Internet Watch Foundation research on child sex abuse live streaming reveals 98% of victims are under 13 years old. Truthfully, I would not necessarily agree with that statistic. It seems disproportionately high to me based on the real cases I am exposed to. Certainly, in many cases the victims are getting younger and younger but what can we expect as a society when a parent chooses to put a 7, 8, 9,10, or 11-year-old who has almost ZERO cognitive reasoning on the Internet where they are being exposed to more than a BILLION followers? Most followers are advanced adults with a great deal more sophistication. Busy parents are challenged because kids know how to hide stuff on the Internet and know how to install private apps on their phones that parents can't see.

The Internet Watch Foundation research goes on to provide some really scary statistics.

96% of victims were girls.

96% showed a child on their own in a home environment.

18% of the abuse was categorized as Category A, which includes the rape and sexual torture of children. (That would imply the child went from a virtual relationship to a live- physical relationship.)

40% of the abuse was categorized as Category A or B which indicates serious sexual abuse.

100% of images had been harvested from their original upload locations.

The first challenge is that for years Hollywood and social media have been gradually lowering any barriers to what is considered moral. I was musing over this one night when a saw a presenter at the Oscars (or maybe it was the Emmys, can't remember) standing at the microphone railing on about how women should not be viewed as sex objects. The woman was standing at the microphone in a dress that was cut down to her naval and up to her ying yang. Really? How can anyone take Hollywood's version on what is moral and decent seriously? And the message is not lost on our children. It is amazing to me how many of our pre-pubescent kids know how to twerk. I even see videos on the Internet of 4-year-olds imitating twerking without understanding what it really represents. This would not be possible on the scale it has currently achieved without social media.

Another example is Teen Vogue Magazine in June 2017 ran an online article on a tutorial how to have anal sex. The magazine caters to 12 to 17-year-old girls. I am not making this up! It even had a diagram in case the girls did not know where that part of their body was. The article went on to suggest this was natural and not even real sex. It led you to believe that you would still be a virgin as this was not really intercourse. As a result, they had millions of viewers. This would not have been possible without social media. Just image the shares this article received between very young kids. What is scarier to me, is that as these young kids shared and shared and some laughed and thought it amusing, they are being categorized in their artificial intelligence profiles as having a legitimate interest in anal sex. Think about the impact of that!

There are several mitigating factors that set the stage for fantasy grooming.

First is the naivety of the parent. As we have already discussed, one of the things that makes a fantasy relationship for a minor possible is the availability of social media where the parent is no longer involved. Technology today has reached a stage where filters and monitors no longer work. I will address this later in the chapter on "Advancing Technologies". Because a parent can no longer really monitor what their child is being exposed to, it should be a <u>very big decision</u> for a parent when they decide to equip their child with a device that can reach the entire world.

There seems to be no danger barometer to calibrate when a minor is in trouble. It is basically trial and error. The challenge for parents is not be overly protective and restrictive or they will have a hard time building trust and openness with their child. Openness is needed for all children to report questionable scenarios where they may be in danger. The opposite end of that spectrum is that without monitoring, without education, without involvement of the parent, the child will be easy to access, isolate and exploit.

Can we really afford to play the odds with our children's lives, with their moral and spiritual identity, and their perception of a healthy sexual relationship?

I BELIEVE THAT FOR MANY OF OUR YOUNG PEOPLE THEIR FIRST SEXUAL EXPERIENCE WILL BE A VIRTUAL SEXUAL EXPERIENCE.

What EVERY person on earth needs to understand is how fantasy relationships work on the Internet. Much of my previous book (*Seduced: The Grooming of America's Teenagers*) addressed this issue. But it is by far the most critical element of any grooming process so I want to readdress it here.

When I make presentations to the public, I often relate a YouTube video that I witnessed. The video was being narrated by adult males who were in a public "Minecraft" video game chat room. They were all laughing and making fun of a little girl that obviously did not know how to maneuver her little avatar. It turns out she is only an 11-year-old and it was the first time she ever played and she did not know how to control her little avatar character in the game.

Suddenly a little boy avatar showed up and started raping the little girl avatar and all the adult males laughed. (Yes, sex is common place in many video games.) Then they realized the little girl was not resisting the rape in the game. They told her, "Honey, run away from him, do something, don't just stand there and take that. Get away from him". Then you heard a little girl's tiny little voice say "I don't know how". Then the little boy character turned her around and virtually sodomized the little girl's character. Then all the adult males laughed.

As I watched this video, I could not help but wonder what the short- and long-term impact this would have on this little girl. Did she realize that she had been publicly virtually raped or was it just another stupid video game and she was not very good at it?

This is very important in the fight against sex trafficking. Literally a minimum of 70% of sex trafficking victims have been previously sexually violated. Are we raising a generation of young people who will be virtually violated and will end up being victimized in real life? Only time will tell.

Certainly, there needs to be a lot more research on the long-term impact regarding when a child's first sexual experience is a virtual sexual experience and it is full of shame, humiliation, and defeat. Will these minors ever be able to have a committed, respectful, giving, normal sexual long-term relationship? We are playing a game of chance with this generation.

I call this phenomenon *"The Chain of Shame."* Many people do not understand how shame works. Shame is different than guilt. With guilt you may make a mistake but it is a one-time event and you can correct it, learn from it, and move on. With guilt, you process the situation as I did something wrong. With shame, it is processed as "I AM WRONG"; I am less than; I am not worthy; I am tainted; I am damaged goods; etc. I believe it is this processing of negative self-images that make some people more vulnerable to a predator than others.

When we recognize that the most likely victims of sex trafficking are foster kids, homeless kids, runaway kids, and pregnant teens, it is easy to see how one's self-image might be affected when a predator is grooming them. Many people are actually born into shame-based environments and from their earliest recollections they feel "less than" or shamed by their surroundings or a family member's behavior.

If there is heavy alcoholism or drugs, parental fighting, even extreme poverty, many people process that as if they have a flaw. Even in quality households and high-income households, if there is not a healthy supportive interaction in family members, young people will have a tendency to blame themselves. Especially if there is a divorce, young people process that as if it is their fault. Their thinking goes something like this: "Perhaps if I had tried harder or been more successful in school or could have been funnier, or skinnier, or prettier or more loving, then maybe, just maybe Mom and Dad would have stayed together".

I also have noticed that with some victims, their mothers had very low self-esteem. I cannot help but wonder if we could provide free counseling early in the process of recognizing this shame dynamic, it might be able to circumvent their child from becoming a victim. Some of the programs I participate in as a lecturer are several Police Departments that conduct rehabilitation programs for delinquent juveniles. One of the things I noticed is that they also provide eight weeks of free psychological counseling to the parents. I have seen some instances where it made all the difference, especially where the juvenile delinquent was a girl.

It seemed like when the mother received coun-seling and gained confidence and self-forgiveness, it was easier for her to communicate with her chil-dren and especially build up the self-esteem of her daughters. It reminds me of the old saying "You can't give away what you don't have". If the mother is oppressed, guilt ridden, and negative, she will greatly impact her children.

Each of these factors increases the risk of being groomed and recruited exponentially. I often tell men in my audiences that they are the key to turning around the trend of sex trafficking. And I mean that with all my heart. I know it sounds sexist. I don't really care. It is the truth.

I believe that at the core of many of our victim's psyche is the belief that they are not worthy and no one believes in them. They believe they are not as valuable as other people. That line of thinking makes them sitting ducks for grooming and recruitment.

I often tell men, that if they will be a strong, moral male with good boundaries, (and boundaries are the key), they have power they cannot even imagine. If they will be moral and learn four words "I BELIEVE IN YOU!", they can change the world of sex trafficking. I share with them, "Go home tonight and learn fifteen ways to say, "I believe in you" and try it out with all the females in your life: especially your daughters, and nieces, and your wife." (I am told it works pretty good with the wife.)

But here is the power of communicating that truth. Think about what a pimp is selling a girl. "I believe in you, Baby. I will take care of you. I will be your Daddy. Those other people they don't care about you". If a girl has never had a father, never had a strong male role model that cared about her, she is infinitely more likely to be an easy target for pedophiles and predators.

In fact, I often think that it is that very concept that makes social media exploitation victims so vulnerable. Think about a 12-year-old twerking on a live streaming app. She is FINALLY getting the attention of men all over the world. They may not really care about her but she has 90 stickers that say to her, "I am good. And men like me". When you put young people on the Internet that have a hole in their hearts as big as the sky, they will go to all limits to make sure they do not lose that approval. And that is how it goes from social media to sex trafficking.

I will always remember the testimony of a survivor of sex trafficking. She shared that she had been raised without a father and her home life was by all accounts truly miserable. When she was 13, this older guy came along and promised her the moon. And even though she knew it was "BS", she desperately wanted to believe. She said in the beginning it was pretty good although he could be demanding. Then one day he told her she would have to sleep with another man as he needed the money. Later it was many men and then she had a quota and there were other women. And then he began to beat her and starve her and call her degrading names and then he would be nice to her again.

This beautiful girl, a survivor of sex trafficking, said something totally profound and I thank her for sharing. She said when it started, she loved him so much that she said to herself, "I will do THIS, but I won't do THAT". Over and over as the beatings continued, and the number of sexual encounters a day increased, she would say, "OK, I will do THIS, but I won't do THAT". She loved him, and feared him, but she needed him and she craved his approval even as it totally devastated her soul. Then one day she said she woke up and realized that there simply was no more "THAT" for her. Today, she has gotten out of the life and stayed out of the life and she is my HERO for sharing.

I could not help but wonder, what if. What if there had been a father, an uncle, a pastor, a priest, a teacher, a neighbor, a friend that simply would have recognized her day to day accomplishments and now and then said, "I BELIEVE IN YOU!"; I am proud of you; You're doing good; You're going to be somebody; We are cheering for you. Just maybe she would not have been so vulnerable. It is worth considering.

CHAPTER FIVE:

TUG OF WAR- REALITY VERSUS FANTASY RELATIONSHIPS

G rooming is all about fantasy. It is true whether you are a child or an adult. What do I mean by grooming? It is when an individual comes into your life and begins to influence your thinking. Before long, you find yourself wanting to please them. You begin listening to ideas that you may not normally be drawn to, and you allow your imagination to run wild. You think about meeting up with them.

You really don't know anything about them, but it is an adrenalin rush to fantasize about all those buried deep-seated dreams you haven't experienced in a long time. You start to feel sexy again. You completely forget about the house payment, the dog going to the vet and the braces your 13-year-old needs. All of a sudden you are alive. Who doesn't love that feeling?

That feeling is the secret to online dating sites. They get a bunch of people to pay money to meet other people. The participants give just basic information. People spend hours culling through the strangers finding one they will like. Once they connect, they begin an online dialogue. And the imaginations run wild. Wow she is pretty. Does he have money? He is standing by a sailboat (or airplane), this guy would be perfect. Bet she likes sex. Almost all of them want to cuddle, hold hands and walk on the beach. I once went on Our Time which is a senior's dating site and it is literally the Sears and Roebuck of horny old men. All of them promise they still have the spark of life.

The same thing happens with our kids. They meet a guy or girl on the internet, through an instant messaging app or video game chat, or a Snapchat or Kik or??? (name any of the thousands of others), and the fantasy begins.

As we discussed earlier in the book, social media is a world that feels like it has no consequences. Technology is making it so we can connect to thousands, even millions of strangers around the globe. Our kids see this opportunity as harmless. They talk to strangers because they can.

It is amazing to me how few people in our society understand the dynamics of online grooming. Because I have sat with many parents whose child is being groomed and have analyzed literally thousands of sex trafficking and sextortion cases, I have come to believe that grooming is not about what the pedophile or predator is saying, but rather what the victims are processing in their heads.

Please forgive the duplication, but I want to refer back to a case that I wrote about in "*Seduced*". There have been similar stories over the years but this case is the best case for all of us to learn from.

This was a case of a successful executive woman with a high achieving exceptional daughter who was 18 and about to graduate from high school. She had a job and a car and a scholarship to go to college. This girl was every mother's dream. (And I suspect she still is).

When the mother heard me speak one day at work, she went home and told her daughter about some of the things she had heard. The girl suddenly started to cry, went into her bedroom, and came back with a passport and an airline ticket to Ireland. This was a Friday night and the ticket was for Sunday morning. The girl said she wasn't going to tell the mother because she did not want her to stop her.

The mother was aware the girl had been playing a game online and chatting with a guy in Ireland, but this girl is sterling. Mom simply thought of it as kind of like a pen pal. The girl herself, even though she is brilliant, did not recognize she had been groomed. The guy in Ireland had convinced her to quit her job and give up school and her scholarship. She had obtained a passport (she is 18) and raised nearly $2000 to go to Ireland.

I will often share this story with kids because I want them to understand how predators operate. I will ask them how I know this was a bad guy. Then we talk about what is an empowering relationship and what is an exploitative relationship. We talk about how she did all the giving and she raised the money and she was giving up her scholarship, so she could please him. (She stayed and graduated.)

It is important to talk to your children about what their relationships look like. If it was an empowering relationship, he would have waited and supported her. But I knew immediately this was a predator because she gave up everything to meet his demands. I hope you will share this story with your kids and grandkids. Think about this. The guy in Ireland was giving up nothing. The girl raised the money. The girl gave up her job and scholarships. It is important to help young people understand that if you are doing all the giving and they are doing all the demanding, it is not a relationship. It is a negotiation and you are going to lose.

When the mother called me to ask what to do, I suggested she try a unique approach. I told her to tell her daughter "If you love him, I am going to love him. If you think he is special, our whole family will like him. So, let's do this. Let's cash in your airline ticket and I will give you some money so we can fly him over here so he can be part of our family. Now tell me everything you know about him."

THIS IS VERY IMPORTANT. Why did I say that? I believe if the mother had said "Over my dead body you are not going to Ireland" she would have lost her daughter. If this girl is smart enough to get a passport and raise $2000, then she knows how to get on an airplane to Ireland. I seriously believe if she had gotten on that airplane, Mom most likely would never have seen her again.

Here is the key to this situation. When you meet an online predator or pedophile, they will normally only give you four or five pieces of information and YOU make up the rest. Because YOU are making it up, it is YOUR fantasy, Your dream, Your new reality. You then set about making it come true. Trust me, pedophiles and predators understand this in spades!

As you meet new people in real life, you quickly come to know their good points and bad points. You see the warts on their noses. You find out they are living in their Mom's basement. You see animal hair on their clothes and learn they have sixteen dogs and cats. You see an ankle bracelet they are wearing because they are on parole. Their reality is right in front of you. You can look in their eyes and read their soul.

Predators purposely don't reveal much about themselves. Not so much to hide their identity but more to give you the room to create your own fantasy so you are not dealing with reality. I believe most predators are not even aware of the details of the fantasy. But it is you, the victim, who creates an alternate world that will motivate you to leave everything you have, possessions and relationships, and pursue your dream.

When the mother asked for my advice and I told her to embrace him with "if you love him, I will love him", that was a version of "I Believe in You". Maybe her judgement is a little clouded right now, but it is important not to reject her. It is a critical point to understand.

WHEN YOU AS A PARENT (OR SPOUSE) GET IN A TUG OF WAR WITH A FANTASY, YOU WILL LOSE!

The point here is that the victim is not dealing with reality and so yelling at them and rejecting them will only make it worse. The victim does not realize what has happened to them. Each and every one of us are wired that way. We will fight to our last breadth to hang onto our dreams. It is how we are made.

What are we to do? I suggest that you find positive ways to ask a lot of questions and help them unpack the situation, so they don't feel foolish. As I mentioned before if you knew someone for nine months in person you would know a lot about them. But when you are dealing with an online pedophile (and sometimes predators in real life) they give you very little information. So, ask fun questions to help the person unpack their fantasy.

"If he is going to be my son-in-law tell me all about him. Is he tall? Skinny or stout? What color eyes? What's his favorite movie? Skechers or Nikes? Basketball, soccer, or football? Does he like to dance? Who is his favorite artist? Is he a steak man or a vegetarian?" Well, you get the drift. The point here is that she will not know. By offering to bring him over and by asking a lot of questions, she is a great deal less likely to sneak off on an airplane. She has your approval and she knows that even though you are aware that she was about to do the most stupid thing of her life, you stand by her. One cannot win a tug of war with a fantasy.

I would like to continue to belabor this point. I often am told by a wife that her husband is having an affair. He plays a video game online every night for four hours; he won't take her out to eat; he won't talk to her; and he isn't interested in sex any more. If you talk to the husband he will say, "No, she is not a girlfriend. She is just a friend I play a video game with for four hours every night". I like to kid my audiences. I will often say, "Let me tell you about this girlfriend". She weighs 110 pounds. She loves to cook. She hates to spend money. And she wants sex six times a night". The wife is not arguing with the husband and the wife is not arguing with the girl friend. The wife is in a tug of war with a fantasy!

The reason I belabor this point and repeat a story from my previous book is that this principle, this concept, is critical for parents and Licensed Marriage and Family Therapists to understand in sex trafficking grooming cases. While the above scenario was about online grooming, this is also true in real life grooming.

The most common scenario is "Romeo Pimping". She is young and he is older and he swoops into her life. Mom and Dad don't like him. He begins by promising her the moon and casually criticizing her family. "Sorry your Dad wasn't there for you last night. He doesn't know what he is missing. You're more mature than other girls and more sophisticated. It is too bad your family is so strict with you. You deserve better. They just don't trust you like I do."

This is a critical juncture for parents to understand. She is building a fantasy that he is directing and enhancing. As parents, you are telling her she is grounded and clean up her room. He is saying, "Hey baby, you're HOT!" Which one of those do you like?

I cannot over emphasize how important it is for parents to understand that their daughter (and sometimes their son) is being groomed. It is important for parents to get themselves and the young person into counseling as soon as possible. It is important that Licensed Marriage and Family Therapists are trained in sex trafficking and sextortion grooming and processes for unpacking fantasies.

At the risk of being redundant, the parents need to work through their differences if any, and build a strong strategy for re-bonding with their child. If one parent is lenient and one parent is strict, the dynamic becomes even more difficult and your success at intervention will be less successful. The parents need to develop a joint strategic plan. In a perfect world there would not be one ounce of daylight between the parents on strategies for dating, online gaming, cell phone use and time away from home.

It would be good to have two to three nights a week having dinner at home where ALL the cell phones are locked in a box and put in the trunk of your car. This is critical bonding time that all too often gets swept away in the normal ebb and flow of raising teenagers.

Perhaps the father needs to find ways to reinforce his approval of his daughter. Maybe they need more family time away at the beach or mountains. Concentrate on rebuilding the importance of the family. Don't over react. Don't nag. Don't reject and judge. Put your arms around her and let her know how important she is to the family. Find things to laugh about.

It is important that you fill her world up so she has less time to communicate with him. You might even try enrolling her in a self-defense class where she can increase her confidence or maybe mother and daughter can try out a summer drama class where she can experiment with her identity.

I am not recommending that you forgo all rules. There definitely needs to be limits and that includes cell phone, meet ups, dress code, and time away from home. Encourage friends to stay over and surround her with positive activity. Try to connect her with a youth group at church.

In the meantime, I feel strongly that when possible, the teen girl who is being groomed by an older male should be connected to a strong counselor as soon as the parent recognizes what is taking place. Preferably, it should be a strong moral male counselor that can compete for her attention. She needs someone she can bond with that will fill that hole she is trying to fill by finding a male who believes in her.

Frankly, none of this is fool proof. I have worked case after case where there was simply little a parent could do. And it becomes even more complex if there has been a divorce or death in the family. The risk factors go up exponentially if she has been previously violated sexually. But I have never seen a case where this situation was resolved without intervention. These kids are worth fighting for and the sooner the better.

CHAPTER SIX:

SEXTORTION-BLACKMAIL WITH A PHOTO OR ILLICIT SEX ACTS

I believe sextortion will be the biggest scourge of this generation until we can educate our young people on why total strangers want a naked photo and what is about to happen to them once they send it. And YES, even Snapchat can be intercepted. National Center for Missing and Exploited Children researches Sextortion and they suggest that the average age of the victim is 14. In my own personal research, the most likely social media platforms used by predators are Facebook, Kik, Skype, Omegle, Musically.

When I have the opportunity to present to students, I often ask them "Who owns the Internet?" The most common replies are "Bill Gates" or "Google" and a couple of smart- mouths have suggested it might be Al Gore. The truth is no one owns the Internet.

Have you ever thought about that? What other things in the whole world can you think of that no one owns. So, if no one owns the Internet, is it private? Almost all kids will tell you: "No, it is not private". I usually respond with "If it is not private, then why would anyone want to send a naked photo on it?"

These are great conversations to have with the young people in your life. Try this on them. "Have you ever thought about what happens when a minor sends a naked photo on the Internet?" No one ever promised you that the Internet was private. In fact, just the opposite is true. Nothing could be LESS private than the Internet. As Americans, we believe we have a right to privacy. We immediately think about the First Amendment or the Fourth Amendment to our Constitution. But it is not called the "U.S. Web". It is called the "WORLD WIDE WEB". It is the wild, wild West on the Internet.

I would like to raise the funding to develop a national documentary, which will be distributed at no cost to schools, to educate our young people about what the Internet is and how it works. It is important for them to understand that not only is the Internet NOT private, everything you send out there on it, potentially can and will be used against you. Few young people (as well as adults) understand how the Dark Web works or how pedophiles form large scale rings pretending to be young girls or guys to get their hands on a child's naked photo that can be sold for hundreds of dollars to thousands of pedophiles in the Dark Web. Pedophiles historically troll through Kik, Snapchat, Drop Boxes, Peer to Peer sites and even video game chat rooms to get their hands on a sexually graphic photo they can drool over and trade or sell to thousands of likeminded sickos.

Before we examine cases of sextortion, let me educate you how this works and why pedophiles are using sextortion on our teens. We will delve into this in a big way in Chapter 11 on child pornography. For now, let's just say that pedophiles and predators are using every ruse possible to access and exploit our kids. Unfortunately, our kids make it VERY easy for them because this is the generation that talks to strangers. This is the generation that is seeking instant and repeated approval from anywhere and everywhere they can get it. They are making themselves sitting ducks for sextortion brokers. In the next chapter we will look at sextortion rings and just how crazy and vile they get. But for this chapter, we will talk about individual predators.

My observation is that predators use a certain level of social engineering in victim selection. We have already established that pedophiles and predators are looking for anyone that is available and vulnerable. That is why it is so easy to pick up kids in online dating sites, instant messaging apps, chat rooms. They are available. You can add to that kids that have low self-esteem, kids who are caught up in a parent's divorce, kids with a lot of time on their hands, kids that want to "prove" they are valuable through gaming chat rooms. They are vulnerable to flattery, praise, and bonding with strangers.

Sextortion is made possible because a youngster hooks up with a stranger who convinces the minor to send a naked photo or to video or to live stream something. Sometimes the young people are so brain washed and sucked in by these predators that they sneak out and meet up with them. It happens to both girls and guys. The results are often catastrophic for both the victim and their families.

In fact, there is a desperate need to educate Licensed Marriage and Family Therapists on how to deal especially with fathers when their daughter has been violated. Few people seem to realize just how devastating it is for a father to find out that his sweet innocent little girl has been sending naked photos or being made a fool of by a total stranger with her complicity. It gets even worse if the encounter results in rape.

While I have never been a father (obviously), I have talked to way too many fathers who are just simply heart broken. They vacillate between blaming themselves and being angry at their daughter while experiencing a profound and numbing sense of loss. Mothers experience this tragedy also but it has been my experience that for fathers this is a life changing experience not only for them but the whole family.

I recall a specific phone call I once received from one of the most devoted and conscientious fathers I have known. He loved his 11-year-old daughter deeply. He had educated himself about social media exploitation and had carefully tried to guide his daughter into the 21st century without being over-bearing. I will never forget receiving his phone call as I was traveling. I pulled over so we could talk without rushing.

He told me that his 11-year-old daughter had wanted a video game called "Hi Puppies". According to the Google promotion, "you can choose your favorite breed", customize your puppy house, and dress up your puppy for a beauty contest. The father told me he looked at it carefully and thought his daughter was a bit old for it, but he was proud of her innocence, and so he bought it for her. He told me in the call that it never once occurred to him that a little kid's game would connect to the Internet and have a public chat room. Apparently, his little girl hooked up with a 19-year male in the video game chat room. The father was calling me from the hospital emer-gency room as the doctors were conducting a rape kit. The loss, self-blame, and devastation this father was experiencing is unable to be conveyed by mere words. Their lives- daughter, mother and father- will all be forever altered. This family, including the father will take years of healing. May God be with them.

Some research statistics indicate that sextortion happens more to girls than guys but frankly, I don't necessarily agree based on the cases that I see. Guys more often get caught up in a video game chat room where the dynamics are such you have a tendency to trust your team mates. Over a period of time, you develop one of those fantasy relationships with a female team mate and you trust her. You begin to think of her as the girl of your dreams and fantasize sexually. One day she sends you a naked photo and now she wants one back. You know better, but hey, she sent hers and how can you look like a schmuck. You send that photo in all your wonderful glory but it turns out she is really a 35-year-old male pedophile in Oklahoma who then sells that photo for $1.00 each to 27,000 guys in the Dark Net. Photos have DNA which identifies the address where it was taken. This young man's life just changed forever. Something very similar happens if you are a girl. You meet a sexy guy online. You bond. You fantasize. You send the photo.

The first thing that happens is that you will start to be contacted by the guy who tricked you. Sometimes if this is a sextortion ring or if the photo is sold to hundreds of pedophiles in the Dark Net, you may be contacted by dozens or even hundreds of these creeps. He (or sometimes she) wants more photos and they need to be more explicit. Now you must be having self sex. You need photos of you having sex with others. Sometimes they know (through live streaming or research) that you have a little sister and they want her in the sex act with you. One little girl recently was coerced to drink her own urine and film it. These demands get more and more vile.

Sometimes they want money: lots of it and never-ending money. You simply will never have enough money to buy them off. They know where you live and they threaten to come over and have sex with you. I know of a couple of families that had to sell their homes and move. They threaten to post it on the school Facebook site or tell your parents. Some threaten to tell others you are gay even if you are not. Sometimes they build websites with your photo on them and make sure you understand that those photos can be seen by millions of people. If it is a live streaming act, they freeze frame it and threaten to post it on YouTube, and other sites.

A child's behavior will change and so will an adult's behavior if they are being sextorted. Girls often start cutting. They become very emotional as they are traumatized. Guys usually shut down and get very quiet. Guys process shame different than girls. Come Hell or high water, they are NOT going to talk about it. These young people will often go to school but they can't stay. That is why I train school counselors and truancy officers to watch for an abrupt change in attendance patterns. Most of these victims can't sleep and many begin to run away without explanation. It is critical to immediately get these kids into counseling if you see this pattern.

The reaction to being a victim of Sextortion is one of the most unique situations I have encountered. I have tried to understand the dynamics. While I certainly understand the components of the situation, I am not convinced I understand ALL the underlying factors. One of the most critical elements of sextortion is that teenagers will go to unbelievable lengths of suffering, threats, emotional torture, and sometimes physical abuse before they will admit to a parent that they are being sextorted. I have watched this scenario play out over and over again. It happens even in some of the finest families who believe they are close and have done everything they could to build open lines of communications.

You would never suspect that some of the finest kids would fall prey to an online predator. My best analysis of what is happening in a sextortion situation is that the teenager will do just about ANYTHING to keep from risking the rejection of a parent based on their sex act. I can't prove it, but perhaps rejection by a parent when caught in a sex act might be a young person's most innate fear.

Teen sex and parents are like oil and water. Teens know the parents "do it" but for a teen to be caught in an illicit sex act is overwhelmingly nauseating. Maybe it is that the teen fears they will no longer be acceptable to a parent or that the parent will explode in anger or that their parents will be so disappointed in them that they will never have the same relationship again. Maybe it is just the fear of losing access to their social media. Perhaps they know in their heart of hearts that the pedophile might just really show up at their front door. Or maybe it is all of the above.

Regardless of the specific fear, what I do know is that time and time again, teenagers will go to great lengths of being exploited before telling a parent. It is my personal experience that in most cases, the teen will NEVER tell the parent until the parent asks them in a straightforward and loving manner.

I know of several cases of highly professional parents who have teens that they have put into counseling because they knew something was wrong. But the teen refused to talk about it even with the counselor. When the parents tried to talk about it with the teen, the kid just shut down or put them off or slid out of the room. What I have found is that it is best to use a straight forward, caring and nonjudgmental question like "Son, I am concerned. Is it possible that you have a naked photo on the internet? Or maybe how many photos do you have?"

The point is that until a teen is questioned in a caring and straightforward way, they will deny, deny, deny until the cows come home.

I could write a book 500 pages long describing various sextortion cases so you could see just how prolific it is. The hard part is deciding which ones NOT to share with you. A couple of weeks ago, I had NINE cases in fourteen days. Three of them were 11-year-old girls and one was a 16-year-old boy who had been coerced into including his 12-year-old sister in his videos. That just tells you the level of devastation these kids feel. I suspect in any other world, this 16-year-old boy would never even consider the concept of sex and his little sister in the same breath. But he was desperate.

One of the questions I often get from parents is "What apps do these guys prefer".

The truth is any and all and every possible technology. Pedophiles love instant messaging apps because you are expecting to talk to strangers. What I want to point out here is that it is NOT the app, live streaming or chat room that is the issue. As long as the communication devices access the WORLD WIDE WEB, there is a chance of a child hooking up with a bad guy. In my research I saw a headline that caught my eye. "Snapchat has a Child-Porn Problem." The article was written by Christie Smythe. In all honesty, that is true of every app on earth as apps are not designed to be the world's policeman. I refer back to Chapter Two and the Great Conundrum.

When I read the story, it was about a 13-year-old Illinois boy who had traded messages with a 19-year-old woman seeking nude photos. He eventually sent her an indecent video of himself. Then he had second thoughts and tried to break off contact. "She" threatened to post the video publicly. HE TOLD HIS PARENTS! BRAVO!!!!

"She" is really a 24-year-old man in California who had victimized at least five other boys. The pedophile said he found the 13-year-old on Snapchat and that Snapchat had become his preferred venue for obtaining child porn. Snapchat has about 200 million users. Law Enforcement will tell you that they cringe when they have a case involving Snapchat because of the nature of the technology and the challenge to catching suspects. Photos and video evidence often disappear from Snapchat before police can find it. Just imagine the challenge to law enforcement as we move full force into vapor ware like live streaming, disappearing video, and virtual image modifications like Fayteq.

When you read this article in full, Ms. Smythe provides us with some really interesting statistics. According to www.bloomberg.com Facebook and Instagram account for 54 percent of the 1631 cases surveyed by University of New Hampshire's Crimes Against Children Research Center. But more private apps such as Snapchat and Kik were the next likeliest avenue for contact of a minor at 41 percent.

I will share with you a broad spectrum of cases to show you how this plays out.

Case 1: Eliberto Jacobo

He was a realtor in Hemet – San Jacinto, California. He was a family man whose wife and kids had no idea what was happening and so they too are victims of this man's exploitation. Eliberto Jacobo set up a fake Facebook page using a photo of a Hispanic girl in a striped dress. He called her Marlissa Garcia. In the fake Facebook ad, Marlissa was into commercial sex (prostitution). She was making money hand over fist, buying clothes, traveling. The implication was that she would show you how to make money in sex, if you were to contact her.

No one knows for sure how many people contacted Marlissa (who is really Jacobo) but the speculation is that it could have been as many as 200. The final number that law enforcement was able to locate exceeded 120 young girls, all wanting to know how to make money. Keep in mind this was a different kind of sextortion in that he laid the bait and waited for girls to find him as opposed to going online and finding the girl. But still it is serious exploitation.

Once the girls contacted Marlissa (Jacobo) online (she/he) would tell the girls that she would set them up with her best customer (which of course is Jacobo). He tips well; He is great in bed; It is just sex; You can see if this is the life for you. No one knows just how many girls showed up and had sex with him, but 17 of the girls were ultimately blackmailed into prostitution. At least three of them were teenagers. Once he had sex with the girls, he would set them down and show them the film they had just made together. Not one of those girls knew they were being filmed during the sex. And the black mail began.

Here is what is powerful about this case. One day I was training in a school doing six back to back presentations. At the end of the second presentation, two cute young girls came up to me, perhaps 15 years old, and handed me their phones. I will never forget this moment. They were laughing and thought it all was just a joke as they said to me, "Ms. Singleton, do you think this is something because we are just playing a game with this GIRL". I immediately recognized the danger and told them it was NOT a game. Think about that. They were a hare's breath away from being violated and having their lives changed forever and they thought it was a JOKE.

I am grateful to God that I was there that day. The long-term consequences on their lives and the lives of their families would be devastating. That is why Million Kids does what they do. I put about 5000 miles a month on my car training the public and much of the training is for kids. I know if you talk to kids they will listen.

Case 2: Marshall Gaudet

Victims called child predator Marshall Gaudet a "monster" before a judge sentenced him to prison. This story caught everyone's attention because he was photographed sexually molesting an 18-month-old child. As sad as this is, there is another story here as Marshall befriended young girls on the Internet and built RELATIONSHIPS with them for months and years. He would then meet up with them and rape them.

Gaudet would find his teenage victims on social media apps where he pretended to be a teenager using the name Josh Rivers. He would build a relationship and gain their trust and seduce them into meeting up with him. Gaudet lived in New York but he had victims all over including Kansas and Texas. When Gaudet was arrested, investigators found a lengthy downloaded manual on how to commit child sexual abuse and not get caught.

Let me pause here and repeat that. Did you get that? He had a MANUAL, probably from pedophiles from the Dark Net. See how sophisticated this kind of criminal activity is? There are published manuals and pedophiles know how to access them. This fact tells you that he was in contact with other pedophiles and while seemingly acting alone, he is communicating and socializing with other pedophiles. At his sentencing, Gaudet was chastised by the Judge because he continued to smirk when statements were made at the proceedings. He showed no remorse.

The teenager that brought the case to law enforcement said she met Gaudet when she was just 13. She met up with him when she was 15 and he raped her. She told her parents and law enforcement about the violation. Keep in mind this started when she was very young and he had three years of grooming her. She truly thought she was in a relationship with someone that cared about her.

Think about the SHAME component for all of the victims. They had built a fantasy relationship with Marshall, not over a couple of weeks, but for months and in some cases a couple of years. The fantasy is deeply ingrained in their identity, so they would have experienced shock and betrayal and sexual violation of the worst kind. The victims would ultimately blame themselves as they realized they had been duped. It gets worse. Not only is this guy NOT the man of their fantasies, he is a monster of the worst kind.

How does a teenager, a teenager without complete cognitive development who is developing her own sexual identity, process this situation? These girls understand they went willingly. Not only willingly, but they themselves created some sort of ruse with their parents: a deception to be able to meet up with the man in the fantasy. How do they sort through and process this as a victim? This experience puts her on a path for lifelong victimization. The chain of shame will keep her bound in thinking: I am tainted; I am ruined; I am not worth anything; I am not like others.

What we don't know is how this will affect a child when the violation is only virtual and not physical. In other words, what about the many, perhaps hundreds of young girls this man had contact with and built a fantasy relationship with, but who had not yet snuck out and met up with him. Will they experience that as shame?

For me, this is the URGENCY to educate our children and teens. We are handing them devices that they have the ability to manipulate in ways parents cannot even perceive or guess.

Case 3: Grindr App

One of the most violated groups of individuals in the sextortion and sex trafficking arena are members of the LBGT-QI community. There simply has not been enough education and outreach for this population. I was privileged to be asked to be a keynote speaker for the Tru-Evolution Organization at the Mayor's Pavilion. I did significant research so I would understand the challenges these individuals face in exploitation. And they are numerous. Even though I have never walked in their shoes or participated as an insider in their communities, I can tell you that I feel strongly that NO HUMAN BEING ON EARTH SHOULD BE SEXUALLY VIOLATED. Period.

During my research quest, I discovered a disturbing story about four men who went on the Grindr app and lured men to a private residence. Grindr is a popular and well know dating app for the gay community. This case took place in Frisco, Texas. Four male individuals are facing up to life in prison and fines of up to $250,000. Purportedly, the men used Grindr to set up dates with four men before they invaded their homes. Officials say the men would then assault their victims, restraining them using tape, and make homophobic comments. They would then steal their cars and belongings. Some were held hostage with a weapon.

My point here is this. Sex and Social Media are a dangerous and sometimes lethal combination. There seems to be no fool proof way to protect yourself once you start to look at the WORLD WIDE WEB as a means of hooking up and finding your new love interest.

Case 4: Tony McLeod

Tony, (38) of Tampa, Florida connected with and exploited two boys from Escondido, California. Tony McLeod had struck up a friendship through online gaming in the spring of 2013. Eventually the online contact turned into phone calls, texts, and video chats in which they discussed their personal lives. The relationships turned sexual and they exchanged sexually explicit photographs and videos.

In this case as reported by Monica Garske in the U.S & World Report, McLeod traveled from Tampa, Florida to Escondido (near San Diego, California) to meet the fourteen-year-old boy and picked him up one day after school. When his parents realized he was missing, they contacted the Escondido Police department who took it seriously. They were ultimately able to link the teen boy to McLeod and determined they were traveling together. They traveled from San Diego to Los Angeles, where they boarded a non-stop flight to Tampa at Los Angeles International Airport. McLeod had booked the teen's boarding pass under the fake name Justin McLeod.

Detectives worked with the airlines, the LA Airport Police, and the Tampa Police Department to track down the pair. When McLeod and the boy arrived in Florida, Tampa Police officers met the airplane on the run way and arrested McLeod. The boy was interviewed by Tampa Police and returned home to his parents in Escondido.

These two boys knew they were talking to an older male about having sex but they had been "Groomed". It appears that the 14-year-old boy even went willingly when McLeod flew out to take them back to Florida. Nothing is stated about what happened to the 15-year-old boy. Perhaps it was his input that was able to escalate this case beyond just another teenager who ran away. What is REALLY impressive here is the police work. Every day Police Departments receive a large number of reports about missing teenagers. There are never enough personnel to handle all of the cases and for the most part, a significant number of teen runaways return home within 24 hours and many are habitual runaways. There must have been something going on here (perhaps the collaboration of the other teen) that alerted Escondido Police Department to react quickly and escalate this. Whatever is the reality here, the Escondido Police Department, the Tampa Police Department, the Los Angeles Airport Police, and the FBI all deserve a standing ovation on this case.

A couple of hours later and this young man's life would have taken a disastrous turn from which he would most likely never recover. It is true that this may not happen to every teen, but to the ones that end up being violated, it is a life changing and serious crisis

There are several critical factors in this case. First, McLeod did not pretend to be a girl. He made it clear he was an older male and that sex would be involved. Referring back to the chapter on Fantasy Relationships, I contend that building this kind of trust and friendship is easy in a video game chat room.

As I will discuss in the Chapter 9 about online gaming, relationship building is a natural progression in video gaming. Think about this. A young person gets an avatar and they live vicariously through the success (or failure) of that avatar. Their score is in front of them at all times and they most often are playing the video game with teammates in their chat room. It becomes "us against them". There is constant pressure to win and keep your score up. And you are talking back and forth with the "mod". It is an alternative world with no consequences. There is just intense competition against the "Other guys". It is piece of cake to groom a young person to trust his teammates, especially, when the groomer is older and better at the game than the child or teenager.

When you analyze this case, McLeod totally understood the concept of winning friendship, loyalty and building trust through seemingly idle conversation in a video game chat room. I also contend that when a minor and adult are both viewing and competing in a video game with high sexual content it is easier to "bond" and deny normal cautions related to sexual encounters with strangers.

CASE 5: Gerardo Perez Uribe, sentenced to 10 years in prison for sextorting 12-year-old girl. Thank you to US Attorney's Office of the

Northern District of Georgia for providing us with this information.

In this case 32-year-old Perez Uribe met a 12-year-old girl on Facebook. He told her he was 13 years old but later claimed to be 25 years old. He asked the girl to send him nude images of herself and she did. Once he received the nude photo, he then took over the girl's Facebook account, locked her out of the account, and changed her passwords. He then threatened to post the girl's nude photos on her Facebook page if she did not send him more. The victim then sent him four more photos of herself which are considered to be child pornography. The girl's parents discovered the photos online and reported it to police.

While this approach to sextortion is somewhat unique in that the perpetrator took over the victim's Facebook account, it is consistent with most other cases in that the first thing the perpetrator will want will be more photos. Usually they want more explicit photos, photos of them having sex with others, photos of their friends and siblings, etc. There will NEVER be enough photos to satisfy these individuals and that is a message that we are NOT getting out to our young people. One photo will ALWAYS lead to more and more. Once you have sent the first photo, you will be their prisoner until you or another victim tells. Many of these kids commit suicide because they cannot face the disappointment in themselves and greatly fear the rejection of their parents. Probably equally incapacitating to teenagers is the fear of losing their cell phone and their social media access.

CHAPTER SEVEN:

CROWD SOURCING - ONE CHILD AGAINST A RING OF PROFESSIONAL PEDOPHILES

C rowd Sourcing is a 21ˢᵗ Century term that takes place when multiple pedophiles come together with the intent of using social media apps, live streaming, chat rooms, etc. to lure in and seduce innocent and unsuspecting minors. It is a relatively new protocol that can only happen because of the convergence of technologies that brings people together with evil intentions and our children become accessible to them. It is an interesting scenario in that often these rings will have 4, 5, 6 and even more pedophiles that have never met in person. They may live in different states and have little in common except the shared enthusiasm for violating children in a particular fashion.

Multiple pedophiles find each other on the Internet and may set up a base chat room where they can share their "finds" and successes. They will often develop a mutual strategy and sometimes give each other names based on their particular expertise in working with minor victims. In one case they gave each other names such as "finder, looper, closer, groomer, watcher, etc." These base chat rooms usually start in the Clear or Surface web where most of us operate. But the pedophiles sell the videos and photos that they are able to collect to thousands of other pedophiles in underground Dark Net pedophile rings. This is called "Crowd Sourcing".

Case 1

According to an article written by Lain Thomas, "Sexploitation gang thrown in clink for 171 years after hunting kids online and luring them in front of web-cams." This group was very organized and had been executing a well-planned strategy for years.

In this Crowd Sourcing group, each sexploitation gang member had a very specific role in the exploitation. The hunter would find a promising young girl and encourage her to join a private chat room, where talkers would engage with her and reassure her. After a suitable period, the talkers would encourage a game of "Dare" and the looper would play a video of a teenage boy engaging in sexual acts to encourage the victim to also strip naked and perform for the group.

All of the gang members that were present would cap (slang for record) the victim's actions to a disk. The watchers would keep an eye on all the participants of the chat room to make sure no one outside the group had joined. These highly compromising recordings would then be shared with others. Many of these recordings were being conducted on a sub-channel of Kik. Author's note: Most parents are not aware that many apps like Kik have sub-channels and many online game chat rooms have sub-chat rooms.

Case 2

In September of 2017, the Department of Justice, Office of Public Affairs released a news release titled: "Four Men Sentenced for Engaging in Child Exploitation Enterprise". Note the term "Enterprise". This was a "Business". The business had a goal of making money and satisfying personal sexual fetishes by preying on very young girls that were provided access to video chat rooms.

The following is an excerpt from the Austin Boro News, the reporter was Bernard Fowler. In this case, there were SIX perpetrators that were preying on pre-pubescent girls. I find it interesting the perpetrators' ages ranged from 31 to 54 so they were not innocent young school guys on a lark. The guys were pros. They all lived in different states (Modesto-CA, Waterford-MI, Glenarm-IL, Diller-NE, Vallejo-CA, and a citizen of the Philippines living in Las Vegas). No one knows for sure how they knew each other, but it is believed they met through the Internet, learned to trust each other, and share similar pedophile fetishes and sexual interests.

"According to trial evidence, between Nov. 16, 2013 and March 10, 2016, Fuller and his five co-conspirators located in different states worked together to lure juvenile girls to a video chat website in order to get them to engage in sexually explicit conduct. The group members predominantly targeted prepubescent girls. The group was active for approximately two years and communicated with each other through "base" chat rooms that were password-protected. In the base chat rooms, Fuller and co-conspirators strategized how to convince minor females to produce child pornography. This strategy included pretending to be teenage boys or girls to help convince the minor females to engage in sexual activity."

This case is a true example of a "Sextortion Crowd Sourcing Ring". Each man played a different role. They would troll through video chat room sites and look for very young children who would be easy to seduce and manipulate (available and vulnerable).

Then they began to build the fantasy relationship with them. Some of the guys would do the finding and initial seduction. Others would threaten the girls if they tried to resist. Once the girls sent the first photo, they were trapped and the men would threaten to destroy them with the photos already sent if they did not provide more photos and more sexually explicit photos. These pedophiles were the loopers and their role was to ensure once a girl was trapped, they would keep producing more illicit photos and videos.

Initially, the girls thought they were talking with a boy their age or a little older.

They would convince the prepubescent or pubescent girls to perform sexually explicit conduct which unbeknownst to them was being recorded, sold, shared and provided to child pornography rings around the globe.

A side note, when a child's photo ends up on some of these global child pornography rings, the photo is out there *forever!* There is no way to get it back or get it off the Internet

I have often speculated that the shock and regret over choosing to send a photo that cannot be retrieved is some of the psychological power of the sextortion process that keeps young kids from telling anyone of their mistake. Once they realize that they cannot get the photo back, the perpetrator ups the ante so to speak, and demands more degrading and compromising acts to be recorded.

The young person realizes that this mistake can NEVER be fixed. Apologizing will not make the mistake go away. A mistake made by a starry eyed fourteen-year-old or an unhappy thirteen-year-old may end up ostracizing them at school, having everyone laugh at them, or look at them as a "Slut". Maybe even more terrifying is the thought that Mom and Dad might find out. As this scenario develops in the teenager's thinking, they may suddenly realize these photos might keep them from getting into a college of their dreams or perhaps the military. No wonder some of these kids consider taking their own lives. I hope this book helps our society understand that Sextortion is a LIFE CHANGING event.

Imagine how easy it is for these guys. They troll through the Internet and they meet young kids and teenagers eager to prove their technical capabilities to total strangers and crave the approval and attention of someone they are FANTASIZING about.

It appears there is no shortage of *pre-pubescent* available on the Internet for the pedophile Crowd Sourcing rings to exploit. It also appears that not ONE of these victims understood they were talking to multiple adult males, let alone an elaborate multi-state affiliation of pedophiles.

Think about this situation from the stand point of the victims. First, many of these young girls have not gone through puberty, so we are not sure what they are thinking when committing these sexually oriented acts. They simply want to please who they think is a cute boy about their age. *Second, at previous noted, not one of the victims understood they were talking to SIX different adult males.* More important, these girl's first sexual experience is one of being a victim. Sex is being used as a weapon in this scenario. These very young girls will experience shame and embarrassment and most likely they will experience punishment from the parent. Their first sexual encounter will be one that will shape their sexual perceptions for the rest of their lives.

If the parents find out, it will also change how the parent perceives the child and will affect their relationship. I talk about this in the next chapter regarding the "Prism of Shame". Our society must realize that these are complex and interactive relationships. It is critical the parent be educated and counseled to help an exploited child work through this violation.

For most of these kids, it will be their first sexual experience. Think of the impact of that statement. Even more, think of how that will shape these young people's perception of a sexual experience which, in this case, is abusive and damaging versus what it should be.

As we have stated, Crowd Sourcing rings are made possible by the convergence of social media technologies that help pedophiles identify and build relationships with like-minded individuals who share a common ideology and/or fetish. Combine the billions of available and vulnerable children who want to be recognized, loved and accepted with the technology given to them by naïve and unsuspecting parents, and it makes one of the most dangerous situations in history for this next generation of young people.

I will be the first to say that most young people will make it through puberty without being sexually or virtually violated. I do not believe a pedophile is hiding behind every bush, so to speak. However, I know from the work that I do and the number of cases I research, this is a serious and dangerous issue for our kids. And we have only just begun. I contend we are playing an odds game. Those kids that are exploited will have their lives and futures changed forever. It is an interesting phenomenon that our society is spending millions of dollars warning about Hepatitis C, STDs, HIV etc. Yet there is no organized effort to merge technology with parents and teens so they are educated to understand how predators use technology to seduce a minor.

Case 3

Here is another example of a "Crowd Sourcing" case. This article was reported by Mark Hicks of the Detroit News. This case was adjudicated in Detroit, Michigan but as far as I can tell none of the perpetrators were from Michigan. Most likely the case started with a victim reporting it in Detroit and due to significant commitment and expertise by the FBI, the case was uncovered across the nation. Great Job, FBI!

The defendants and subsequent sentencing are as follows:

Terry Kovac, 49, Las Vegas, Nevada, sentenced to 37 years in prison.

Felipe Dominguez Meija, 31, Springdale, Arkansas, sentenced to 41 years in prison.

Noel Eisley, 38, Wapinger Falls, New York, sentenced to 35 years in prison.

Eric Robinson, 42, Duluth, Minnesota, sentenced to 34 years in prison.

Bret Massey, 47, of Portland, Maine, sentenced to 32 years in prison.

William Phillips, 39, Highland Park, New York sentenced to 33 years in prison.

Over a period of four years these men posed as teenage boys on social media apps and chat rooms to lure underage girls or "Captures" as they called them. They played different roles and were successful in building the girls' trust and convincing them to engage in sexually explicit conduct on web cams. The group recorded the activities and shared it with each other. Note: this article does not suggest these recordings were sold in the Dark Net.

Working together and playing various roles, the group recorded tens of thousands of sexually explicit videos with minors, some as young as 11 years old.

The FBI has so far identified 48 victims but they state that there are well over 100 victims.

I would like to point out that this is often the scenario in Sextortion cases. The FBI reports the ring had tens of thousands of sexually explicit videos with minors and yet they can only identify about 100 victims. This tells me there are really THOUSANDS of victims that have been violated but have not been located or identified. The article does not make the scenario clear but my guess is that <u>not one of these victims realized they were talking to six different men</u>.

I believe that with advancing technologies like Live. Me, Periscope and the Dark Net, Crowd Sourcing is just getting started. The potentials for mass victim exploitation as third world countries come on board the Internet will reach a scale and scope we are unable to fathom today, even with our wildest imagination.

Case 4

As I am writing this book, yet another "Crowd Sourcing" Sextortion Ring is being brought to justice. In this case the perpetrators were:

Arthur Simpatico, 46, Mississauga, Ontario (Canada)

Jonathan N. Rodriguez, 36, West Hollywood, California

Michal Figura, 35, Swarthmore, Pennsylvania

Odell Ortega, 36, Virginia Gardens, Florida

Brett Sinta, 25, Hickory, North Carolina

Caleb Young, 38, Olmsted Falls, Ohio

Daniel Walton, 33, Saginaw, Texas

William Phillips, 39, Highland, New York.

Christian Maire, 39, Port Dickinson, New York.

When I read articles like this I am always amazed even though I work in the business. First, I want to thank Anthony Borrelli at PSBA Borrelli for reporting this case and providing us with the details so we can educate others.

Consider the perpetrators. They are from 25 to 46 years old. These men are not precocious teen-agers on a lark. These are adult men who are full of conniving and ill intentions towards their victims. They appear to simply not care or are not willing to acknowledge that they are destroying the lives of risk-taking young kids.

In fact, I would be willing to speculate that many of these pedophiles believe it is the kid's fault for being so easy to manipulate and seduce. That is how pedophiles think for the most part. They will blame the victim. They will swear up and down that these young girls wanted to be found or they would not be playing on the Internet making themselves available. As disgusting as this line of reasoning is, I do agree that we must help parents and teens understand the dynamics of Crowd Sourcing sextortion and do everything possible to educate the public so innocent kids will no longer fall for the sextortion seduction. That is the purpose of this book.

According to this article, these adult males targeted minors several times a week via chat-based websites and had been conducting these activities since 2012. According to one article I read on this case, they actually kept a spread sheet of names, interests, and successes in achieving photos that were shared amongst the other perpetrators. That spread sheet tells me they are truly dedicated to the cause of exploiting young people. Their targets were 13 and 14 years old girls. Christian Maire personally recorded a child porn video of a girl who was 15 years old. Christian is an attractive middle age male with a wife and two children and yet he seemed to have a considerable amount of time and interest in exploiting young teenage girls.

Using the online group chats, the perpetrators organized strategies for targeting victims. The group of perpetrators apparently met regularly in a separate on-line chat room to develop strategies and celebrate their successes and share their videos and photos of the naked minors engaging in various sexual activities.

The Crowd Sourcing Sextortion Ring was very dedicated to the cause of exploitation. They actually gave each other names which I find interesting because they were similar to the names in the other case we just discussed. The terminology and modus operandi of the two groups complete with the names assigned to each perpetrator role is the same. However, there is no duplication of the names of the defendants or nothing to indicate that the two groups knew each other. Still, I am highly suspicious that there is some unacknowledged connection between the two groups.

This makes me believe that there is a "Sextortion Crowd Sourcing Manual" somewhere floating around the Dark Net very similar to the "Pedophile Manual" that is used for child pornographers in the Dark Net. It is amazing how organized these pedophiles can be.

"Hunters" sought girls to bring to the website and alerted other members of the online chat group.

"Talkers" were in charge of conversing with the girls and getting them to engage in sexual conduct.

"Loopers" played previously-recorded videos depicting a male minor chatting or performing sex acts in a chat room. Then the Looper posed as that male minor when speaking with the girl.

The purpose of this "Crowd Sourcing" chapter is to educate parents and teens alike about the scale and scope of sextortion rings. We no longer can be content to deceive ourselves and say that this is just some hyper-hormonal teenage boy seeking to trick a young girl he may have a grudge with or conversely have a crush on. **This is serious organized crime and our kids are the target.**

One of the most important strategies in educating our children so they do not become victims of sextortion is to *never talk with strangers*. I know it is an old and dull saying. It is important to sit with your child and look at some of the cases on the Million Kids Facebook page and discuss with your son or daughter how all of it happened. Reassure them that you are counting on them to be a leader and not fall prey to exploitation.

Reiterate with your child that the most effective means of making sure they never get exploited is simply say "no" and move on. If predators do not get a quick and easy response to their bait, they will move on to an easier target. It is a time-consuming process to groom a child. If your child is not easy to manipulate, they will move on to someone who is easier. Remember the hierarchy for a predator is AVAILABLE and VULNERABLE. Don't make it easy. Teach your children to not be low hanging fruit.

I remind you, when we put a 9, 10, 11, 12, 13, 14-year-old minor on the World Wide Web, we are opening the door to many people you would not invite into your living room. And we are counting on our children to have the INNATE ability to recognize danger and evaluate complex criminal situations even when their frontal lobes will not be completely developed for many years. Add to that the fact they are often hormonal and each and every one of them is seeking attention and approval. It is a total powder keg of risk. When it goes wrong is when I get involved. It is truly sad. These are lasting and forever experiences which will form the character of the child for a lifetime.

CHAPTER EIGHT:

PHANTOM RELATIONSHIPS AND THE PRISM OF SHAME

T his just might be the toughest chapter of all to read. However, I believe this is cutting edge psychological exploration and a concept that is critical to understanding the impact of the depths of shame victims of sextortion and social media exploitation endure. Additionally, I believe that future research will show that in a significant percentage of sextortion cases there will ultimately be a correlation between becoming a victim of sextortion and a victim of sex trafficking.

The reason for this concern is that a recent study by Florida Atlantic University and the University of Wisconsin-Eau Claire suggests that as many as five percent of America's teenagers are victims of sextortion. Researching the number of teens in the U.S., it appears there are approximately forty million young people, so that would mean that at least TWO MILLION of our young people could become victims of sextortion. The grooming and shaming process of sextortion are similar to how perpetrators seduce and groom victims of sex trafficking.

Multiple research studies across the U.S. suggest that a minimum of seventy percent of the young people engaged in commercial sex (prostitution) in the U.S. were previously sexually violated. I fear that we are opening the doors to an absolute epidemic of sex trafficking over the next decade if we do not address the psychological grooming processes involved in sextortion and more important the multi layers of shame and trauma that sextortion victims experience.

IF WE DO NOT ADDRESS THE TRAUMA PROCESS OF SEXTORTION, WE WILL BE CREATING A SHAME BASED SUPER HIGHWAY FOR SEX TRAFFICKING VICTIMS OVER THE NEXT DECADE.

We just finished the discussion of sextortion in chapter six. Perpetrators and pedophiles will hook up with our kids in a wide variety of ways. Maybe it is an instant messaging app like "Kik" or a chance encounter through receiving a Snapchat, or maybe there is a perceived bonding experience with a team member through an online video game chat room. Regardless of the means of the hook up, as we have previously discussed, a "fantasy" relationship begins with someone the minor has never met.

The victim begins to build a sexually oriented relationship online with a new-found friend. As we talked about the perpetrators, they can be a male pretending to be a female or a female pretending to be a male, or it can even be a large ring of "Crowd Sourcing" perpetrators. All are seducing a child by pretending to be the child's fantasized new love.

149

Regardless, the victim engages in a sexual fantasy with someone who is perceived as trustworthy. Perpetrators are usually much older and more sophisticated than the young people they are seducing. For the most part the minor is easy to manipulate. Remember our conversation about "Available and Vulnerable".

Most of these young people are looking for love and acceptance in all the wrong places. Without education and supervision, they are easy prey for much more mature and polished pedophiles. All of us want what we cannot have and the lure of a stranger is intoxicating and exciting. "Someone out there really thinks I am great". As we talked about in the first chapters these young people are unable to perceive the consequences.

The reason I call these "Phantom Relationships" is that this victim will self-violate and be exploited by someone they have never met. Many victims will also meet up with their predator and in those cases the level of exploitation is beyond comprehension at times.

When a child is sexually abused by a family member or someone they know, there is someone in the room with them. There is the sense of "Touch" and it is obvious the violation is being forced or coerced on them by another human being. There is someone to point to as the monster.

In this chapter I want to deal with the unique phenomenon that is expanding around the world called "Self-Violation". What happens is the child falls in love with their fantasy and builds a trust in this phantom relationship. Maybe the young person thinks it is a hot rock star or movie icon or just a wonderful caring boyfriend or sexy and attractive new girlfriend. The perpetrator will ultimately convince the minor to go into their bedroom (or other secret place) and strip, or masturbate, and/or commit a wide variety of sex acts on themselves. They are encouraged to film it in live streaming or take photos or videos and share it with the perpetrator. The assumption on the part of the victim is that they are pleasing their phantom lover and it is confidential and will be kept between them.

Once a photo, video or live stream is shared with the perpetrator, the perpetrator then reveals that the victim has been duped and the blackmail begins. While we talked about the process of sextortion in the previous chapter, what I want to explore with you, the reader, is the psychological journey that each victim is forced to endure once they realize they have been trapped.

Put yourself in the place of a fourteen or fifteen-year-old boy or girl who is the victim in this scenario. First of all, this may be their first sexual encounter and it is about to get REAL UGLY. At the very least, they truly thought another human being found them attractive, sexual, and valuable as a unique individual. Now they realize they are trapped by a monster that never cared about them and did not find them attractive. More importantly, they very quickly realize their lives could be ruined socially and they are heartbroken. They most likely will panic.

I believe there are several levels of trauma that this victim is experiencing. One of the first is the fear a parent will find out. The horror of having a parent catch them red handed in a sexual self-pleasuring act just might be the greatest innate fear a young person could have. Quickly that moves to the realization that NOBODY really cared about them or found them sexually attractive. Then the first emotions may well be feelings of self-disgust and feelings of being ugly and undesirable.

Once the pedophile has the photo or illicit image, they almost always show the image back to the victim. However, rather sharing it in a loving and caring manner, it is now presented as a threat and announcement of disgrace. They begin to demand more images. They want more images that are even more sexual in nature, and start to demand scenes that are vile and demeaning. They threaten to expose the first images to their school friends, their Facebook page, their parents and on and on. They usually want images of them having sex with others or photos of them doing degrading and humiliating acts. They may demand money and a lot of it.

These cases reach a level of pain and erotic violation that we as normal human beings can barely bring ourselves to process. In most cases, the victims will try over and over to negotiate their way out of it. As I mentioned earlier, I have known of cases where the victim was forced to photo themselves licking a toilet bowl or drinking their own urine. In many cases the victim will have two or three years of photos that the perpetrator is demanding and reposting so others can see. BUT STILL THEY WILL NOT TELL A PARENT.

What is going on here psychologically? I am not a trained therapist and welcome input from those professionals in this field. However, I have dealt with way too many of these cases and have reached some level of understanding of what a victim might be dealing with.

First, I think there is a secondary trauma component to this. Think about it. In this situation the victims have been lured into self-violating believing they are pleasing the object of their fantasy. But then the perpetrator shows them the photos/videos that the victim created and uses them to shame the victim. The victim is not only experiencing first-hand the raw shame of being exploited, but they are viewing themselves in an out of body experience and JUDGING themselves as if they were someone else looking at it. I believe it is the same kind of trauma that victims of sex trafficking experience that makes it so difficult for victims to find self-forgiveness and recovery.

In exploring this concept, I spoke with my Pastor, Kerry Decker at Compass Christian Church in Riverside, California. Kerry often counsels men and couples on the impact of shame. Here are his comments.

"It's interesting how the 'Prism of Shame' differs from other forms of child abuse.

With other forms of abuse, the perpetrator takes advantage of a trusted relationship and inflicts harm upon the child. In typical abuse, the child may perceive escape from his or her abuser as being impossible or very difficult. Someone in the house or family may be the one inflicting the harm. The victim may not see escape as being possible.

The roles of abuser and victim are clear. With the 'Prism of Shame', these lines get blurred in the mind of the child.

The relationship with the perpetrator is, at least initially, voluntary. And, I believe that this is the key difference. The "perpetrator" is actually the victim. This is what I think magnifies the shame. With typical abuse, victims can say, "How could you do this to me?" And they can get to the place where they banish the perpetrator from their lives.

Not so with the 'Prism of Shame'. When the victim is also the "perpetrator," there is only haunting self-recrimination: "How could I do this to me?" And while as victims we often feel contempt for our perpetrators, it is different in the 'Prism of Shame'".

"THE PRISM OF SHAME: The object of my contempt is me."

Apart from God's grace and forgiveness, I cannot separate from my sin. What makes the 'Prism of Shame' so insidious is the blurring of the lines between victim and perpetrator, as well as the difficulty that the victim finds in escaping the memories of the wrongdoing that "I did upon myself." I appreciate Kerry's insights on this subject and believe it is right on the mark. Thank you, Kerry for sharing with us. You can contact Kerry at KDecker@Pacbell.net.

Few people are looking at the impact of multiple layers of shame and the subsequent psychological prison pedophiles place on victims in the crime of sextortion. It is a crime that changes a child and often their family forever.

In case after case, the child will do anything to keep from telling a parent. If you will follow Million Kids on Facebook you will see a new case of sextortion almost every day. There are simply too many for me to include in this book. The tactics for tricking and luring the young people and the ingenuity exhibited by pedophiles simply boggles the mind. Unless we educate our kids about sextortion, we stand to lose literally millions of kids' futures.

I believe sextortion will change a child's sexual identify for the rest of their life. It will challenge the young person to have healthy self-esteem and recognize their own self-worth.

Think about this. For most of these kids, their first sexual encounter may be one not only of shame and grief, but will prohibit them from ever seeing sex as a healthy encounter with someone you trust never to hurt you. In order to have sex in a loving committed relationship, an individual must have trust that the partner is not going to violate them.

The other element of being able to be in a healthy relationship is having a healthy opinion of your own worth. Sextortion victims will be robbed of all those critical elements unless they can find a trusted counselor where they can confess and work through the multiple levels of trauma and self-judging they have endured at the hands of someone they have never met.

There is also an additional critical element going on in the world of sextortion to which our society seems oblivious. I hope to change that with this book. When a father or mother discovers the photos/videos of their child in a sex act they are shocked, disgusted, angered, and experience a multitude of other emotions. Nothing in our society is preparing parents and grandparents for what is taking place with our kids.

This is especially difficult for parents if the child has self-violated where there is no one else in the photo. Having taken these calls from parents, I can tell you the grief is real. In a recent case where a pre-pubescent child was coerced to insert objects into her body and film it and send it to the predator, the father simply could not be consoled. Think about the impact of this scenario. The father and mother had bought the 11-year-old girl the phone. She had met up with a pedophile and wanted to please him. She has not gone through puberty and does not have a solid understanding of what sex is and what it should be. At the risk of being a wench I will say it one more time, when you put a child on digital devices before you have the sex talk, other people will educate your child about sex and you are not going to like it.

As I recall this situation, it broke my heart. It happens in this work. These were wonderful people and good parents. For nearly three hours the father and I worked through his emotions. From self-blame (what was I thinking giving her a phone), to anger, then despair, and vindictiveness, to rejection and blame and on and on. Remember these cases are very difficult for the child. There is NO ONE in the room with the child violating her. She is self-violating in the hopes of pleasing her new friend.

I believe it is absolutely critical that we train Licensed Marriage and Family Therapists across the nation and church counselors and pastors and school counselors and as many people as possible so we can work with the families of these victims. This father will never look at his daughter the same. The little girl with some counseling will probably recover although there will always be an emotional scar. Her sexual identity has changed forever. But the father is grieving the loss of innocence of his daughter.

I BELIEVE OUR SOCIETY IS NOT PREPARED TO HELP FATHERS AND MOTHERS GRIEVE THE LOSS OF INNOCENCE OF THEIR CHILDREN.

It is possible that this will be an entire new segment of counseling. This little girl might get counseling and get better, but if the father does not work through his anger and grief at the situation, he will one day throw her a "Zinger" that will set her back for ever. If there was ever a time that little girl needed the complete and unequivocal acceptance of her father and mother it is right at this moment and going forward. But a pedophile came into their lives and stole their precious daughter's soul. It will affect the marriage. The parents may begin to blame each other. It may affect the intimacy of the marriage. The father may withdraw or become more aggressive towards his daughter. In many ways it might be easier for him if there was a pedophile he could see and blame, but in this case the girl is in the room by herself. But she is only eleven years old. There is layer upon layer of emotions that must be worked through.

SEXTORTION IS NOT A SINGLE VICTIM CRIME. IT WILL AFFECT THE ENTIRE FAMILY

As technology advances and the world becomes interconnected, we are going to see a significant increase in the number of cases of sextortion and also a greater advancement in the nasty nature of the sexual violation that pedophiles will require of victims.

Let's talk about the game of dare currently going around the globe. It is called "MOMO". MOMO is a ghastly looking creature that is part chicken and part woman. Remember with animation the sky is the limit when we begin to create images that will intrigue our children. While MOMO is certainly an interesting character, I am not concerned about the physical nature of the image. In the future, there will be hundreds of different characters like MOMO. It is the technology I am concerned about and how it allows a total stranger to come into a minor's life and literally take control in less than twelve hours. In many cases, someone that a child has never met AND WILL NEVER MEET will come into their lives and convince them to take their own lives in a very short time.

Momo has many variations but for illustration sake let me lay out how one version works. MOMO (woman/chicken character) suddenly pops up on your cell phone or digital device. They challenge you to a game of dare. Sometimes a calculator appears on your phone and they tell you to pick a number, any number. The minute you do that you have unknow-ingly opened a door to a virus. That virus goes directly to your address book and your photo album. Predictably, many young people have naked photos or sexual images hidden away in their phones.

The victim plays a round or two of dare and then tells MOMO they are through. They don't want to play anymore. Then MOMO brings up an image that the victim has been hiding and the blackmail begins. They threaten to send that photo to everyone in their address books. This is literally happening all over the world.

When I speak in schools, almost a third of the kids know about MOMO. (Interesting the parents, teachers, counselors and principals do not until we train them.) I share with them how this technology works. The bottom line for kids is this. Not only is it important that you do not send or receive naked photos but they need to go home today and clean out all illicit photos they may have on their phones. There literally is no safe haven in any digital device any more.

What is unique about games like MOMO is that in a very short period of time, someone they have never met and will never meet will come into their lives and take control. In case after case, these kids become imprisoned in their own fear and shame. They simply do not seem to be able to ask for help or admit that they have made an egregious error.

The game very quickly progresses as the predator behind MOMO takes over the victims normal thinking and seemingly possesses and controls their every action. In several cases these kids have ended up jumping off a building as they are mentally trapped by an animated character blackmailing, shaming, threatening and controlling a perfectly talented and quality individual that has entered into the 'Prism of Shame'.

I want to return to the conversation about the psychological process the minor experiences. Whether it is from a game like MOMO or another technology used by a predator, the 'Prism of Shame' has taken over a minor. It will involve a photo or video taken by the child or teenager. The illicit photo/video is shown to the victim and the victim is forced to now look at themselves in a sexual activity. But now the victim judges themselves as being involved in an embarrassing situation.

The photo/video they are viewing may have originally been made in a loving setting but is now being used as blackmail and the context for the viewer changes. They may even have an additional layer of shame as the photo may involve sex acts with a friend or lover and they will process feelings of fear and rejection that they have compromised someone they care about.

In addition to understanding the "Fantasy" factor in grooming, I believe there are two critical factors that are a force multiplier when pedophiles recruit kids on the Internet.

The first is ISOLATION. In what other world would a child or teenager be allowed to function in absolute isolation without parent or friends that could observe their behavior and tell someone when they are making decisions that might ultimately be harmful to themselves or others?

Predators and pedophiles get that in spades! One of the first things predators will do is to try to either turn the child against a parent with lines like "Don't tell, this is our little secret" or "I am sorry your folks don't understand you" or the converse, they will shame the teenager with the idea that they are a sissy if they can't make decisions themselves.

It has long been known to psychologists and law enforcement that pedophiles will seek to separate a child from a parent so they can gain complete control over their prey and minimize the risk that a child will tell of the abuse. The world of social media and online gaming chat rooms is a perfect environment for accessing the child and then begin to isolate them from all things known and comfortable to the child. It is about CONTROL.

As long as pedophiles can isolate a child or teenager from outside influences, then they have control over their prey. This is true in domestic violence cases, sextortion cases, and victims of sex trafficking. One line of thought I have often pursued is that when a teenager (or child) is given a phone, the minor immediately understands that this is the one and only activity where they can maintain autonomy because they understand that the parent knows a lot less about the device, apps, chat rooms than they do. In a sense it is at that moment, they begin to enter into an environment where every teen begins to live their lives the way THEY want to live it, chat with whomever they want, say whatever they want, do whatever they want, and become friends with whomever they want. Minors understand that it will be difficult for the parent to really know what they are doing.

As I look at case after case of sextortion and online game exploitation, it becomes apparent that the primary recruiting environment was the many times the predator and victim communicated and bonded in complete isolation without the influence of the parent or other family members.

THE DANGER OF ISOLATION IN A GROOMING ENVIRONMENT CANNOT BE OVERSTATED

The predator will take complete control over the minor's life to the point that other members of the family including Mom and Dad will not be able to offer influence but will also be perceived as the enemy. The only possible antidote to counteract this situation is immediate and intense therapy for the minor and separate therapy for the parents.

One really tragic example of this is a television show I viewed recently on Investigation Discovery

Channel (to my best recollection). It was the story of 14-year-old Breck Bednar in the U.K. who had met 19-year-old Lewis Daynes in an online video game chat room. He ultimately brutally killed Breck. The story relates just how important Breck was in their family and how they doted on him and supported him in his every activity. The family is obviously a fantastic family who did everything within their power to protect and guide Breck.

According to the story, Breck met Daynes in a video game chat room. Almost immediately Daynes began to isolate Breck from the rest of the gamers. He would suggest that the others were juvenile and not as smart as Breck. Daynes was able to isolate Breck and then he created an environment where Breck began to idolize Daynes believing his was older, more sophisticated. Breck even said several times he wanted to be like Daynes.

Breck's family seemed to do everything right. They listened in to the chat room and began to limit Breck's playing time. They tried to talk to Breck about their concerns and changed their family outings so they could all spend more time together and less time on the computer.

Eventually they actually took the electronic devices away and they saw a major difference in that Breck seemed to return to his normal energetic and humorous self. What they did not know was that Breck was secretly in communications with Daynes. Daynes continued to indoctrinate Breck trying to turn him against his family. What was apparent was that Daynes still exercised tremendous influence and control over Breck's thinking.

In the end, Breck told his family he was going to be sleeping at a friend's home in their neighborhood but he secretly travelled to see Daynes after months of secretly talking to him through online gaming forums that no one knew about. Daynes ultimately stabbed Breck in the back of the neck near the brain stem, killing him. This appears to be a pre-mediated event as a month before the event he bought duct tape and other items online to facilitate the attack. Daynes had even given Breck a mobile phone and sent instructions by text on the lies Breck should tell his family so he would be able to sneak out and see Daynes the night of the murder.

If you know of anyone who has a teenager that is being manipulated or controlled or unduly influenced by an individual online, please seek help immediately for both the potential victim and separate counseling for the parent. Don't give up. Stay with it and do everything you can to break the isolation and access between this child and their predator. While it is very difficult to watch, I highly recommend that you Google "Breck's Last Game: Story of Teenage Boy's Murder". It is a powerful documentary regarding online grooming.

In this tragic story, I believe ISOLATION was the key to gaining Breck's trust and taking control of his life. It is a true travesty for the entire family. My condolences to all involved.

In addition to fantasy and isolation, I believe the power of ANONYMITY is the other primary factor involved in the grooming process. Let's face it, we all would do things we normally would not do if we thought no one would know and we would not get caught. For teenagers (and younger), there is an innate sense of total anonymity on the Internet. It is their world. They immediately assume some air of superiority and autonomy because it is not a real world and so they can do whatever they want, at least that is how it feels at the time.

This anonymity really comes home to me when I speak in schools. I explain to kids about Photo DNA and that every email, text, chat room conversation that goes out around the world in the surface web is being scanned by Photo DNA. Then I explain that others can intercept their naked photos sent to a boyfriend or girlfriend, they look at me in total disbelief: maybe even a little fear but perhaps that is my imagination. My point is that kids believe it is their world. They immediately ask, "What about Snapchat photos and drop boxes?" Yes, they can and will be seen by others. When I tell kids that nothing is private on the Internet, they sometimes become indignant. Some don't believe me. Their immediate reaction is that "They have a right to privacy". I explain to them that is U.S. kind of thinking based on the First and Fourth Amendment. But this is not called the "U.S. Web". It is called the "World Wide Web".

Why is this important in a discussion on grooming? Because I believe that many young people take and send naked photos because they BELIEVE they are private and they won't get caught. Very similar to the previous discussion on Grand Theft Auto, there is a sense of autonomy by our young people that it is their own private little world and they can do what they want and there will not be consequences.

It is that very thinking that makes it so easy for total strangers to convince our kids to go into their bedrooms and commit sex acts on themselves or strip naked and film it and send it to people they have never met. It is the perceived autonomy that strips us of our inhibitions and good sense.

I believe this really gets magnified in online gaming chat rooms. Think about this. You get a user name. No one knows who you are really unless you tell. You build a fake character (avatar) and you use your Bitcoin account (which is anonymous) to dress up your guy or girl avatar and you begin to live in an alternative world. But you still have a personal ego that is being played out in your character.

This is my point. If you have a fake name, and you have a fake character (avatar) and no one at home is watching what you do on the Internet either because they don't care or can't understand it, then you have all the autonomy in the world. For a teenager, that FEELS like they can live in a fake world, do what they want and no one will know who they are and what they have done. In their mind, it does not count because it is not real.

The problem is that the decisions they make in that fake world may one day be brought to light and used against them. It is naïve. One day, they will pay the ultimate price as their "Deed" is no longer really anonymous at all. In fact, it will be used against them in ways they could never dream possible at the moment they decide to take a risk because no one will ever know. Education is the key to breaking anonymity.

For starters, I want to make a documentary to educate kids BEFORE they get in these situations. I want them to understand this is taking place all over the world. WE MUST REMOVE THE ISOLATION in the sextortion scenario. I believe education of parents, teens, schools and the public is critical. That is why I wrote this book. If we talk about it, I know kids listen. We must help kids understand they are not the only one. There is a way out; They can get help without rejection; And that it is a crime and something must be done.

I also believe that it is critical to educate kids all over the world so they will not be easy prey. An informed kid is much less likely to be recruited or exploited. Certainly, there will be kids that will not listen or who are so confident they won't be a victim that they will most likely be the first victims. But my experience is that most kids will pay attention and many kids will help us lead a national campaign.

If we can make it much harder for pedophiles, then they will have a harder time being successful.

If you want to write to me with your ideas, you can do that at Opal@!MillionKids.org.

CHAPTER NINE:

ONLINE VIDEO GAMES CHAT ROOMS - AN INCUBATOR FOR GROOMING AND BONDING

Talking and writing about online gaming and video game chat rooms is always a bit tricky. Kids freeze up and begin staring daggers at me. Parents freeze up because they "know" in their heart of hearts that they have little understanding of the world in which they let their kids play. So, let's take this head on.

Games are here to stay. Schools are setting up coding classes and gaming design classes within the school. There has been much research done as to whether gaming and the accompanying side effects will be good or bad for our kids in the long term. As usual there are two sides of the story.

Gaming as a whole has many benefits for our kids and today any child that is not at least playing some sort of game will be deemed to be disgusting and undesirable by their peers. As in most things there is a spectrum of harms and benefits and that is really true of gaming.

At a minimum, gaming teaches hand eye coordination, strategy and decision making, teamwork sometimes, and learning to lose as well as win. Gaming when done in moderation, with healthy games played with only individuals you have met in person, can be a great way for your child to develop. The problem is that few games really fall into that category.

One of my concerns as a Christian (without being too radical) is that many games are set in the Occult and Sorcery or combating other Gods like Zeus. As I researched the types of games, I was amazed to see the number of games where you actually play

God. I cannot help but wonder how the REAL GOD feels about teaching our children it is OK to play God. But I digress.

Those of you that hear me speak in person will often hear me say that playing a game is much different than taking a young person to an off color or violent movie. In a movie, you may hear bad words, see sex and violence etc. but it is happening to that character and everyone goes home.

They dynamics of a video game are quite different. In a video game you may compete in a world of violence and sex but it is not happening to a movie character. In a video game, the player develops an avatar with a very specific identity. Kids spend much of your hard-earned money buying "Skins", tattoos, equipment and building an identity for their avatar. Most important is that the acceptance and/or rejection of their avatar is based on their score.

Think about what this means. If you are not able to be a top scorer the pressure from the guild/mod can be enormous. They will put the heat on you to get your score up or go play with "girls" or someone of lesser status. That means each player lives vicariously through the success or failure of their avatar.

For teenagers who are building identity, or who may have low self-esteem, or who has not yet developed strong cognitive decision-making skills, they can be extremely at risk of being groomed, recruited, exploited, and manipulated. We ALL want to be loved and admired and accepted. The world of video gaming is one of the most competitive environments a child can exist in.

For some kids, their acceptance and rejection are everything. Without parental involvement and parameters, they will spend long hours trying to develop their skills, even overlooking their chores and school grades. It is a well-known fact that in many Asian countries, video game addiction has become an epidemic even to the point of having live-in addiction recovery centers for thousands of teenagers. I am not suggesting that this will happen to every teen. I believe that most teens will engage in video gaming about as much as a parent will allow them.

One of the real problems going on in our society is that many teens spend long hours unsupervised. They are caught in a divorce situation where there is a war going on between Mom and Dad as to who HAS to take the child this weekend, or both parents work, or there simply is not a two-parent household. Video gaming is a great way for these kids to escape the drama or fear of rejection or at a minimum a lack of inclusion. The end result is that they create their OWN world and it is a world where a parent does not know how to get in.

One of the most critical factors in analyzing the dangers of online video gaming to a child is based on several factors: 1.) The age, gender and maturity of the child 2.) Amount of violence and sex in the game 3.) Whether or not the player will be interacting in a public chat room or in a private chat room with only people they have met in person. 4.) If they are playing a game that has a lot of sexual images and/ or sexual interaction with a character.

Let's examine these factors. One of the first concerns with games is that kids are playing online games younger and younger. Nothing is preparing them to understand the dynamics in which they are competing. A child who is seven, eight or nine has ZERO cognitive reasoning skills to stand against an adult predator they cannot visualize. Very young kids have been taught to use their imagination and they usually play in a fantasy world. Therefore, gaming works perfect for them as they are comfortable with living with nonsensical and animated worlds. It is that very factor that makes them so easy to access, groom, recruit and exploit by a pedophile because they are so trusting.

Most parents never even consider their child might be exposed to a pedophile through on-line gaming until it happens to their child or someone they know.

READ THE INSTRUCTIONS. IF IT SAYS IT CAN BE HOOKED UP TO THE INTERNET IT WILL ENABLE A PUBLIC CHAT ROOM.

We can talk ad nauseum about the amount of sex and violence a child will be exposed to in video games. There have been many studies on the subject of violence in a video game and whether or not it will inspire a child to act with violence in real life. I believe these studies are biased or very narrowly focused. Many of these game makers are generating hundreds of millions of dollars every year and they are certainly going to commission studies in their favor.

Like so many things in life, I don't think this answer will be fitted nicely into a research study. There are so many mitigating factors.

How strong the child's personal identity is, their self-esteem, their self-worth.

How easily they can be influenced by emotion.

How competitive the child is.

How strong a child's spiritual foundation is.

How many hours per day the game is being played by the child

The type of violence in the game

How frequently the child is seeing violence.

Whether the violence happens to others or is focused on their character.

Whether there is sex in the game and whether it is interactive sex that you pay for or participate in.

One of the challenges for a parent in making decisions on a video game is that they have a disease called "FEAR OF AVATAR". In what other world would a parent turn their child over to the influence of outside strangers for hour upon hour without having met that person?

Truthfully, when you allow a child to play a video game you have never researched or played, you are allowing total strangers to talk with your child about sexuality, violence, spirituality, evil, sorcery, and many other things where it would never occur to you to ask for outside opinions. The answer is: Get yourself an avatar and play the game with him/her at least intermittently. You may not be good at it. It is not the point. Playing a video game with a teenager is a great way for a father/grandfather and mother/ grandma to talk about digital morality and explore the impact on the child.

You may not be aware but MANY, let me repeat, MANY, MOST, A LARGE NUMBER, etc. of video games have sex in them. If you Google "Teen Porn Games" there are 727 million search results. In fact, in some games, sex is a weapon. What a great opportunity for a father or grandfather to engage in the conversation.

I believe that most parents are still thinking of sex as something two people who are married are sharing in a loving and respectful relationship. I challenge you to get involved with your child's video game and take a long look at how sex and sexual relationships are portrayed in video games.

It is no accident that most female characters are portrayed as 44D's and many games have prostitutes. Most video games contain foul language and a lot of it. And of course, almost all video games give points and victories for killing. What is interesting is to give your youth group or teen group a survey on attitudes about online gaming and chat rooms.

Most of the kids will tell you that sex on the internet is not really sex. I usually respond by asking them why they just paid $50 to have virtual sex with the prostitute and then killed her to get their money back. In one group I surveyed, one fourth of the youth group told us that sin on the Internet was not really sin because it was not real.

That does give one pause for cause. I believe my Bible says something different. But few parents even realize their child is thinking that and even fewer yet see that attitude as an issue.

The real challenge in video gaming is how to protect your child from total strangers. It is easy for total strangers to reach your child, build trust and friendship and loyalty. It is easy for that child to develop an intense need to receive the support and approval of these individuals they have never met. I can think of few scenarios in our world that offer so much access to kids who normally would never be in danger of being groomed. This is especially true for teen boys.

To give you an idea how this plays out. Imagine a 13 or 14-year-old boy playing Fortnight, Minecraft or World of Warcraft. One day a really hot girl joins the mod. She seems to like him and he is starting to respond. Remember "available and vulnerable"? It works the same with boys. They tweet, they text, they chat and they play the game night after night. He wants to impress her and he is willing to take chances to do it. One day that cute young thing sends him a naked photo and now she wants one back.

Well he knows better. He has heard about this stuff but somehow this one is different. They have been talking for weeks. He is love. Maybe he is in heat. Things are looking good. So, he decides he can trust her. He takes that photo in all his wonderful glory and sends it off to her.

But it is really a "HIM". He is trapped. That pedophile sells that photo to thousands, sometimes hundreds of thousands of pedophiles in the Dark Net. This young man's life and the life of his family has just changed forever. There is no fixing it.

We talked about this in the Sextortion Chapter but I wanted to revisit this in the Gaming Chapter because that is how most young males are trapped. Game chat rooms are like the "Garden of Eden". You can have anything you want so almost every one of us will select the "Forbidden fruit". Game designers know how to make it all so irresistible. Pedophiles understand that to the max and for them it is a different kind of game. They love the seduction process. They love finding that weak child (or adult) that is easy to manipulate and seduce. Most of the pedophiles that play in online games have tens and hundreds of victims. They almost always want more photos and they better be really erotic and degrading.

I want to remind the parents reading this chapter that there will NEVER be an end to this without parent and law enforcement intervention. The reason they want more photos is that they are being traded, sold and shared with thousands, even hundreds of thousands of pedophiles in the Dark Net FOREVER. Once the first photo is sent, you will never get it back. You will see in the next couple of chapters some of these photos are sold for $1.00 each and to 20,000 to 50,000 people in a child pornography ring. I remind you that most photos have GPS and the pedophile can determine the address where the photo was taken. That means the pedophile could theoretically show up at the victim's home. Pedophiles will use that information to harass and terrify the victim. There have been some cases where the family had to move because of the sexual harassment by total strangers once the first photo was sent.

The idea that all it takes is ONE child sending ONE photo seems to be a concept our society is not willing to look at. I HOPE TO CHANGE THAT. I welcome your support in doing so. We must educate parents and teens. The answer is easy. NEVER EVER post anything or send anything on the WORLD WIDE WEB you would not print on the front of your church bulletin or your town's newspaper. If it is not "out there", it cannot be used against you. If you are tongue tied or have trouble discussing this with your child then either 1.) Don't put them on a game or 2.) Sit down and read this chapter with them.

There are two more concepts that are critical in understanding online video game chat room seduction. Try to visualize the scenario that is taking place when you place a child in a video game that has sexually oriented characters. This is especially important if your child is in their sexual development years.

Let's say your 13-year-old son is playing a game like Game of War. The game is very sexual. Recently I had a 14-year-old young man at a school tell me the game was really "Raunchy". His words, not mine. He told me it was full of adult pornography but he was addicted and could not give it up. He is FOURTEEN. I think what kind of man will he be when he is 16, or 18 or a father or husband. But more important what I want you to consider is his VULNERABILITY to a predator.

He is fourteen and immersed in competing against other teams while he is watching adult sexual images and needs and wants to support his teammates who are competing against other teams. So, a person (male or female) he has never met in his chat room is also looking at these sexual images.

VIDEO GAME CHAT ROOMS ARE AN INCUBATOR FOR GROOMING.
WHAT YOU HAVE IS A HEIGHTENED STATE OF AROUSAL

ON A SEXUALLY DEVELOPING KID WHO WANTS AND NEEDS THE APPROVAL OF A STRANGER WHO IS ALSO VIEWING SEXUAL MATERIALS WHILE CHATTING WITH YOUR CHILD.

It is an interesting phenomenon that few people are looking at this challenging situation. It really is not a radical concept. It is simply an understanding of the environment in which hundreds of millions of kids play every day. Fortunately, most somehow survive without becoming victims of sextortion.

However, it is also possible that it is early in this societal experiment as we are just now understanding how many kids are being impacted emotionally in the critical stages of their sexual development. This subject never makes the headlines of the evening news. I refer back to the Department of Justice report mentioned in the "Sextortion" Chapter where we know that sextortion is affecting at least three million kids in the U.S.

At the risk of sounding like I have gone off the edge completely, I believe there are very few research studies that are looking at the long-term sexual attitudes of these game players or how social media is changing what is moral and acceptable in our society. I had one girl in a high school tell me that she "had" to send her date a naked photo or he would not go out with her.

Many kids will tell you that sex on the Internet doesn't really count as sex because you are not engaging in physical sex with others. But in a way you are. When you have online sex in a video game, others can see it and you are more likely to talk about sex as part of the game. Furthermore, with most online sex in a video game, sex is a WEAPON where you get points and can increase your score.

I contend that this is one-way sex. And while you may experience a release, you have not had a meaningful, respectful interaction with another human being WITH INTIMACY. In fact, when the sex is shared with team mates, it is sex as a conqueror, sex as a dominant player, sex as a weapon used for victory.

Only time will tell if and how this will affect intimate relationships long term in our society as we are raising a generation of young people in competitive, animated sexual combat. Most parents are oblivious to it.

If you follow Million Kids on Facebook you will see case after case where young people are seduced in video game chat rooms. I have selected a couple that I thought might get your attention.

Case 1: Kristen Aragon and Melissa Goelz

This is a case of a 14-year-old Oklahoma boy who was playing and chatting in an online video game Xbox Live party with Kristen Aragon, 35 years old from Farmington, New Mexico. Twice she persuaded the minor to send photos of his penis. And they began to text regularly as she groomed him. Aragon told the boy she lived just an hour away but she really lived eight hours away in Farmington, New Mexico.

The talk turned sexual and they exchanged photos. The boy said he originally told Aragon that he was 17 but later told her that he was really only 14. Aragon told him that she already knew how old he was and where he lived. Aragon told the boy that she wanted to have sex with him.

Aragon brought her friend Melissa Goelz and together they made the eight-hour drive from Farmington, New Mexico to Oklahoma City where the victim lived. Aragon and Goelz arrived at the teen's home in the middle of the night and picked him up. Aragon told him "he would never be back". Aragon then drove him back to New Mexico where he was sexually violated several times.

The victim's dad reported him missing and police were able to track him to the two women using the ping on the victim's phone and through messages on his Xbox. Officers were waiting in Aragon's driveway for her and Goelz when she arrived home.

PLEASE NOTE: We thank Gina Tron who is the author of this report on the Los Angeles Daily News. At the time of the writing of this book, this case has not been adjudicated so we want to stress that the charges in this article are ALLEGED until such time as the defendants have had their day in court and received due process.

Parents ask me regularly which games are safe games? What about Fortnight, Minecraft, GTA V, Game of War, League of Legends, World of Warcraft, Roblox etc. The rule of thumb is that ANY game that is connected to a public chat room will make your child "available for grooming". A person can play in a game with a private chat room or no chat room, but a young person who does not have adult cognitive reasoning will never be able to hold their own against a multitude of adult males they need to please.

If you are questioning just how real this is, Google an article "Authorities Warn That Predators Are Targeting Children on Fortnight." This article was authored by Sarah Gangraw and she can be reached at www.instagram.com/sarruhhhhh.

Fortnight is just about the hottest selling game in the world right now. It is impossible to play Fortnight without interactivity with individuals in chat rooms because it is all about "Taking Out" total strangers. Each game starts out with 100 players who are picked off until there is a lone victor. The game heavily relies on communications, as many users form alliances to stay alive longer, which can be par-ticularly concerning for parents because their chil-dren are exposed to strangers. Many people have reported that their children were offered money for sexual favors.

A mother from England learned her son had been groomed by an online predator. She said her 12-year-old son was asked for naked pictures and was offered $50 to perform a sex act and was being asked disgusting questions by another Fortnight user. In the same article, a teacher who asked to remain anonymous said that many of his 11-12 year-old students have had similar encounters.

I read another article with the same inclinations but this time the game was Roblox. This article was written by the organization "Protect Young Minds". In this article a Dad found vile messages from a predator in a Roblox game that his 8-year-old son was playing. "The Roblox chat feature allows strangers, and potential pedophiles to directly contact and communicate with young kids. If your child allows a stranger to friend him, the friend be notified whenever your child is playing."

In this particular case, the Dad decided to get an avatar and play the game. OUTSTANDING! I wish more fathers would do this. He posed as an 8 year-old-boy and entered the game room. He was quickly approached by two strangers who asked his age and gender. When he responded that he was an 8 year-old-boy, they asked him to follow them into their house and bedroom (in the game). They then asked him to lay down on top of them and they started with sexual movements.

I thank "Protect Young Minds" for publishing this story. It follows on the same message that I share. First, 8 year-old-children are too young to play on a game that is connected to a public chat room. Secondly, when you (or a child) are playing a game that has a public chat room, you are surely going to encounter some very vile and nasty people looking to hook up and violate any young person they can seduce, trick, lure or otherwise exploit.

In looking at my vast stack of research, I try to determine which case is the best illustration for you to see how prolific this is. Honestly, I have hundreds of cases. I suggest you follow Million Kids on Facebook and you will see on average four to five of these cases every week. EVERY game that has a public chat room will be a danger for a young person. No exception. If your child is under 14, I suggest they play only those games that have a private chat room. This way they can enjoy all the great attributes of gaming but not have to worry about being seduced.

There are two other issues I would like to address about gaming. Some young people and adults are becoming total gaming addicts. It takes over their lives. They become aggressive and difficult. They give up school and work.

Online gaming addiction is a very real thing. If you have a person in your life that is addicted, please take it seriously and get them help. One of the best books I have ever read on this subject is written by Dr. Andrew Doan, PHD, MD. The book can be ordered at Amazon and the title is "*Hooked on Games*". He also operates a website "*RealBattle.org*". Dr. Doan is a Neuroscientist and one of the global leading experts regarding online gaming addiction.

If you should have a person in your life that seems to have completely turned their lives over to online gaming or perhaps they have changed their personality completely, there is reason for concern. Maybe this individual is living in an alternative world or they have become radical in a particular line of thinking. I want you to be aware that some chat rooms in online gaming have sub-chat rooms. These are private, invitation only chat rooms with members for specialized groups like ISIS, Home Grown Violent Extremists, and hate groups of all kinds.

Pay attention. If you have a young person in your life, I would suggest that you get yourself an Avatar and have them show you how to play. They will appreciate the attention and more important, you can let them know THEY are worth your time and worth fighting for.

Finally, I want to discuss a new trend that is taking place in the gaming industry that I find down-right scary. It is called "THE FREEMIUM MODEL". Historically, parents would spend their hard-earned money buying their child the latest video game. At a minimum, it provided the parent some sense of understanding what games their child was playing and gave them an opportunity to engage in dialogue about the game. The parent then provided the minor with a credit card to buy some "Skins" to upgrade the child's avatar in the game.

When a new player joins a game, they select an avatar and then buy tattoos and equipment and give it a name. The players compete vicariously via the avatar. Early in the game, the player is not so skilled and the buying of skins helps them raise their score until their skills get better. The average player was spending about $89.00 a year on upgrades for their avatar.

However, in 2017, some game makers switched to the "Freemium" model. That word is a combination of "free" and "premium". Instead of paying to buy the game, the game makers began to make the games FREE to the player. This means that many parents are not even aware of what games the minor has. More importantly, the game makers build obstacles inside the game, which make it nearly impossible for the average player to progress without "buying" a solution to get around the obstacle and continue playing.

Since game makers started the "Freemium" model, reportedly the average player went from spending $89.00 per year on avatar upgrades to spending $550.00 every six months to buy upgrades and get around the implanted obstacles in the game.

The "Freemium" model puts poor and financially challenged young people at a great disadvantage and I contend at great risk. In our area we have already seen two cases where pedophiles preyed on poor kids. The predator put the pressure on the kid to get their score up and move around the obstacle because they were holding back the team from beating the others.

In the cases I encountered, the predator told them to get their score up or leave the team. The player told the predator they had no money to buy their way around the obstacle and the pedophile offered them $50.00 in Bitcoins if they would send a naked photo. They did and the sextortion began. Where is the outcry against the game makers for putting our financially challenged kids at risk? The silence is deafening.

CHAPTER TEN:

THE IMPACT OF ADVANCING TECHNOLOGY ON CRIME AND CRIME SOLVING

O ne of the primary reasons I titled this book "Societal Shift" is because of the profound impact of technology currently being realized on crime and crime solving. Few people realize how technology is not only changing our everyday lives, and the future lives of our children, but how it is currently changing Law Enforcement's ability to keep families safe from global and local pedophiles, cartels, and organized crime.

I have long felt that a primary reason that America has enjoyed more freedom and more financial success than most other nations is based on the fact that in the 1920's and 1930's, our nation developed law enforcement entities to take on the Mafia and organized crime.

In the early days of our nation, we welcomed thousands of immigrants (legally) who had dreams of starting a new life in a land of the free. Along with them came mobs, cartels and mafias, along with a few homegrown ones in the U.S. that preyed on poor immigrants demanding rent or taxes and threatening harm to their loved ones if they did not comply.

The stories of Elliott Ness and Al Capone were legendary to old timers. But of course, few young people today have a clue who these folks were and the impact they have had on our society today. This generation enjoys complete societal freedom to insult their government and their leaders and earn as much money as they can in any legal fashion. They do not have to live in fear of some mafia goon coming along and shaking them down for "taxes" or threatening them with death if they publicly share their opinions.

In some countries today, if you post negative comments about the government on Facebook, you can go to jail for years or be expelled from the country. If you did that in the U.S., half the population would be in prison.

My point is, that by stamping out the extortion, mob violence, and underground economies earlier in that century, this generation is allowed to live in the land of the free without fear of a shakedown or violence against our loved ones by cartels, gangs and mafia. If you look around the globe at third world countries struggling to survive, you will see entire nations, whole societies, are bound and gagged (metaphorically) by some criminal enterprise.

Countries like Mexico, Turkey, Columbia, Italy, Russia, Sudan, Venezuela and on and on have underground economies. Many citizens of those countries are experiencing extreme violence and even incarceration for non-compliance. It is no wonder so many people are trying to illegally cross the border into more ordered societies where there might be some protection through rule of law.

Certainly, America has their share of crooked politicians but our rule of law and due process allows us to file complaints, develop investigations, and charge even the highest government leaders with corruption. That is simply not true in many countries where the top cop IS the criminal.

Why does that matter in a discussion of the "Societal Shift"? It is because we are about to be a world without boundaries. As the entire world is connected by technology, then so is crime and crime solving. In fact, a world without borders for our kids is also a world without borders for criminals, pedophiles and global organized crime. More criminals can now access our kids and adults than at any other time in history. Add to that, the easy and prolific access to the Dark Net and we are about to see global criminal enterprises on a scale and scope hard to articulate.

There are several critical factors impacting this scenario.

1.) Rather than protecting the innocence of a child, we are handing them devices so predators will have total access to our kids. We used to tell our kids "Don't take candy from strangers" but now we hand them a cell phone (candy) so they can talk to the entire world.

There is no protection on who can reach our child except a cautious parent saying "You be careful on that thing, you hear?" Frankly, this is happening sometimes before the child gives up their pacifier.

As you will hear me say many times in this book, the child is a technology wizard and parents are techno handicapped. Unless we create a generation of young people who are FULLY educated to understand the seriousness of the world in which they now live, we will pay the consequences. Hopefully, most of the youth will survive unscathed or with minor infractions. But truthfully, unless we undertake a global education revolution, a portion of our young people will be violated.

2.) Technology advancements have reached a stage that neither law enforcement nor parents can keep a child safe on the Internet. As I write this, our kids have apps with disappearing videos and photos, encrypted messaging and chat rooms, vaporware like live streaming and "poof "it is gone. We have crypto currency which for the most part is anonymous and non-traceable, and then we have virtual reality and artificial intelligence that will join art and pornography and change evidence in a crime scene.

Already we are seeing crimes where the person's photograph is altered with other faces or animated images. All of this describes the challenges that parents will have in monitoring their child's social media behavior. Parents will be able to see there is communication going on but not be able to read it. They might be able to tell they accessed a live stream room but not see the images.

More important, how do you investigate a crime if you cannot get a search warrant or track the money? Under today's crime solving protocols, there has to be a reasonable expectation of corroborating evidence that there is a crime for a judge to sign a search warrant. Obtaining search warrants take time. Social media applications are instantaneous and often immediately disappear, thus the term "*Vaporware*".

3.) Equally important in the discussion of crime and crime solving is the impact of global privacy and law enforcement protocols and policies. While this is a discussion that could cover an entire book, suffice it to say that law enforcement investigation and prosecution of criminal activity globally could be one of the greatest challenges to this generation.

For example: If you have a 58-year-old pedophile in Milwaukee who is live streaming sex acts of a 13-year-old girl in the Philippines, the challenge will be in determining where is the crime? Certainly, in the U.S., sex involving a 13 year- old is against the law, but the age of consent for sex in the Philippines is 12 years old. If the parents consented and the 13-year-old complies, is it legally classified as Pedophilia? Only time will tell.

Then you have privacy laws. In 2018 Europe implemented the GDPR, (Global Data Privacy Regulations) Act that will greatly limit access to personal data. It is believed that even with search warrants, it will be difficult to find out the "Who is" or who actually owns a domain that might be involved in displaying child pornography. We will wait to see how all of it plays out, but for now, many global cyber security companies are setting up shop in Romania and Australia where they are less regulated and more committed to breaking the privacy of an Internet user if there is a reasonable belief that a child is being exploited.

It is hard to overstate the importance of this development. We know that a world without borders for criminal enterprises means that a vast majority of crime will entail both victims and perpetrators who live in multiple countries with multiple law enforcement jurisdictions.

As we progress through the next decade, one of the great discussions that will be ongoing is the individual's rights to privacy and how that is juxtaposed against the government's role in keeping society safe from criminal activity. Already, many large cities have installed street web cams and some are experimenting with facial recognition connected to public webcams. These systems are already in place or being installed in many airports around the globe. Many security systems are being transitioned with facial recognition or thumb/finger printing devices (called biometrics).

Governments around the globe are amassing mega data collection systems which are being exchanged and overlaid with other data. Corporations are building your artificial intelligence profiles and sharing that data with other corporations and assumedly some government agencies.

Facebook collects, sells and trades your every search, your every click, your every location. Think about this. Facebook has never charged you a dime but they are nearly a TRILLION-dollar company. We have reached a stage where your government and hundreds of private companies know if you have dentures, birth control, inflammatory bowel disease, and hormone replacement therapy. They probably know more about you than your spouse!

In a recent update of the Golden State Killer case in California, this information collecting reached a whole new level. Law enforcement has been working on this case for nearly forty years. It is believed that the Golden State Killer is responsible for at least 12 murders, 45 rapes, and 120 home burglaries from as early as 1970 but they have never been able to solve the identity of this prolific criminal.

Recently Cold Case Detectives accessed some of the older DNA samples from a crime scene years ago and submitted the DNA samples to a "public" family ancestry company to see if they could learn more about the perpetrator's ancestry. They had previously submitted the perp's DNA to a multitude of government DNA databases but there was no match.

Think about the impact of this. You the consumer want to find out if you are really Scottish, or Irish or German or switched at birth. So, you send in your DNA and you get this great little report finding out you are really Italian and you are all excited. Never once does it cross your mind that YOUR DNA is now in a community database and law enforcement might access that database to solve cold cases of murder or track down a questionable relative you have been suspicious of for years.

Well, the unique and novel approach by law enforcement worked! When Investigators submitted the decades old DNA, they found a relative of the suspect was a match. The suspect's DNA was not in that database. They contacted the relative and began to work their way through the family tree.

It was ultimately confirmed that the Golden State Killer was 72-year-old former police officer Joseph James DeAngelo. I want to point out at the time of this writing this is ALLEGED in his charges as he has a right to due process and has not yet been convicted.

4.) Another challenge to crime and crime solving in the "Societal Shift" is the way law enforcement agencies are organized and funded. In many of the sextortion and social media exploitation cases that I have researched or been involved with, there are multiple perpetrators and often hundreds of victims living in various states and sometimes multiple countries.

The result will be that law enforcement may be called to a perspective victims' home where a police report is made. For example, let's say there is a 14-year-old girl who has been talking on the Internet with a young man she believes to be 16 and he was able to convince her to send multiple naked and sexually illicit photos to him. Note: Cases like this often occur multiple times a week in my world.

Law Enforcement is jurisdiction defined. In other words, crimes committed in Riverside, California are first investigated by law enforcement in Riverside,

California. Typically, this case would be investigated by a Deputy who reports to a Sergeant, who reports to a Lieutenant, etc. If there is evidence that the perpetrator is out of Riverside County then, most likely, the case is referred to state or federal authorities. My point here is that the case will first be seen as a victim in Riverside but truthfully, unless it is particularly egregious, the case will be noted, the victim will be cautioned about the Internet, and it will not go much further.

However, in many of these cases, the victim is often speaking with more than one perpetrator and most likely not in Riverside. As we saw in some of the previous cases, it is not uncommon to have sextortion rings made up of multiple perpetrators with a wide range of ages and living in many different cities and most likely they have never met. What is even crazier is that the victim does not understand they are actually being groomed by multiple perpetrators.

More important to understand is that this case is being brought to law enforcement through boots on the ground doing old fashioned law enforcement work. However, the actual crime is being perpetrated in multiple cities by multiple perpetrators and therefore, with a little luck, will ultimately be referred to a federal agency.

There is also a significant likelihood that the photo of the minor victim is not only being circulated between multiple perpetrators but it is being sold hundreds, perhaps thousands of times in the Dark Net. The challenge here is how many of these cases will actually be developed by local law enforcement and connected nationally or internationally so that all the perpetrators will be located, documented, charged and prosecuted.

Most law enforcement officers I know care deeply about the victim and want to prosecute as many perpetrators as possible. But crime and crime solving are changing. Not only is the scale and scope growing exponentially, but the vast range of jurisdictions involved in the cases because of living in a world without boundaries for perpetrators is making it increasingly difficult for law enforcement under current state and federal structures.

Here is the challenge. A world without borders will mean that a LOT more of the cases will be federal cases. The obvious implication here is that the U.S. will need a vast increase in federal law enforcement structures and agents to be able to deal with crimes that would normally be handled by local law enforcement. Additionally, it will be critical to set up national and global databases that are shared within ALL law enforcement agencies. Having the free sharing of databases between ALL law enforcement organizations in the U.S. and globally may truly be one of the greatest challenges of all time as historically, organizations are territorial and guard carefully their Holy Grail.........the almighty database.

Having said that, I believe you will see an inversion of the crime solving protocol.

By that I mean that currently a crime or potential crime is identified by a citizen and reported. The information is provided to law enforcement that investigate and determine if there is enough evidence to identify a perpetrator and prosecute. As we discussed, if it is believed that this crime might be outside the jurisdiction of local law enforcement, it will then be referred to the appropriate federal or state agency.

I believe that much of that process will be reversed in future crimes. In fact, the crime will probably be identified through online data in some law enforcement skunk works buried in the basement of a federal building somewhere and fed to local law enforcement to investigate and decide if it is a viable case.

This model suggests that much more law enforcement funding should go to the state and federal level and be focused on creating technology driven investigations. Subsequently, it will be referred to the local law enforcement jurisdiction. It will change budgets; it will change structures; and most important, it will change the amount of resources allocated to a local crime and subsequent investigations.

5.) Most likely, the greatest challenge to future crime solving will be the ability to work within legislation, federal and state laws and follow privacy policies and protocols based on the ever-advancing technologies. As we previously identified, even today it is difficult to get a search warrant and crack encrypted messaging and encrypted chat rooms.

To get a search warrant requires probable cause. It requires some level of evidence of what law enforcement is seeking that is very specific. With Vaporware such as live streaming, the evidence is instantaneously dissolved and very difficult to track. Encryption requires hours of work and it is difficult for law enforcement to break the code. Even crypto-currencies, like Bitcoin, are often anonymous and non-traceable. There also is the challenge of getting a search warrant in the Dark Net when in fact you have no idea what you are going to find and where the information is going to lead.

6.) Another technology that will change crime and crime solving is block chain technology. Block chain is a bit challenging to define for the lay person but let me make a very surface level approach at it. Right now, data that you gather through your local computer is either stored on your hard drive or parked out in the "Cloud". Obviously, data that is stored on the "Cloud" is easier for others to hack and access. So when criminals and pedophiles collect illegal images such as child pornography, they usually store them on their desk top computer or on a series of back up data storage devices such as thumb drives, disks and drop boxes. The photos are often shared on "Peer to Peer" networks between pedophiles and they often exchange photos in secret chat rooms in the Dark Net.

When law enforcement intercepts images they believe to be CAM (child abuse materials, also called child exploitation materials or child pornography), they get a search warrant and arrive at the pedo-philes' location(s) and begin confiscating their hard drives and storage devices. Block chain technology will make collecting evidence that much harder. Block chain is in essence decentralized computing. Rather than storing the data in one centralized location like a hard drive, the data is sent out through a series of "Blocks" that are "Chained" together.

In reality, what is really happening is that computer owners all over the world agree to loan out their unused capacity within their computers to be a "Data miner". Most of the time this is electronically transmitted and the person has no physical involvement. With 5 G networking being installed all over the world this will facilitate the rapid transmission of data between data miners, seemingly at the speed of light. Almost instantaneously, when a person using block chain starts a data entry transaction, it will move rapidly from block 1 to block 2 to block 3 and be bounced from data miner to data miner in a fashion that is hard to follow or comprehend.

At this writing a normal block chain will have 2400 blocks in a chain from start to finish. I assume in the future it will fairly quickly grow to 4800 blocks in a chain or even 7200 blocks in a chain. The beauty of block chain is that it is transparent. The tracking of the data through block chain will be quick and efficient and easy to validate as the transaction is not complete until all blocks in the chain are connected, validated and finalized. If they cannot validate the validity of each block in the chain from start to finish the transaction is voided.

When you first hear the concept, you assume that it will be EASIER for law enforcement to track transactions because the block chain is transparent and traceable. However, there is a catch. No one knows the identity of WHO started the first block chain transaction and who ended it. Let me explain.

Suppose someone makes a $500 deposit through a block chain transaction. You will be able to track the deposit from the first block chain all the way through to the 2400th block chain. So, the transaction is transparent. What is not transparent is WHO made the deposit and who made the withdrawal. Those are anonymous. That will make the tracking of these transactions very difficult for law enforcement. In many legal cases, the most important piece of evidence is tracking the flow of money.

Block chain is simply a transmission and book-keeping process. It can be used to transmit all kinds of data including financial transactions, inventory records, and even images such as child pornography. Block chain is currently being used by many, many major financial corporations, retailers, and industry because of the vast amount of data that can be transmitted and the transparency in record keeping. Where it will be a challenge for law enforcement is how do you get a search warrant and how do you determine who is transmitting the child pornography and who is receiving it, or who is depositing the money and who is withdrawing it.

New Technologies are helping Law Enforcement in the fight against evil.

Some of you may feel I am extremely negative on the future because of technology. Au Contraire! Nothing could be further from the truth. I have been combating sexual exploitation of minors and adults for over ten years and I have witnessed the evolution of technology that is being developed to catch criminals all over the globe and yes, even criminals using the latest technology to do their deeds.

For the past couple of years, I have had the pleasure of working with Adam Mosher of Global Intelligence Solutions in New Brunswick, Canada. Adam has dedicated his life to developing technology that will help law enforcement find and investigate child abuse materials all over the globe. It is truly cutting edge and being beta tested by federal child sex task forces globally. I am proud of individuals like Adam who care enough to focus their time and energy to get ahead of the bad guy. It is not easy.

Another super hero who is investing in technology to combat sex trafficking and child pornography crimes is Ashton Kushner and his organization Thorn. Ashton has put his money where his mouth is. Many celebrities talk a good game about charities but Ashton has invested in many technologies that expedite law enforcement's ability to identify criminal activity and has developed algorithms that help both federal and local law enforcement quickly isolate cases of human exploitation where the victim might be in danger.

Homeland Security is a master at pursuing Internet crimes against children and using technology in ways that can identify millions of pedophiles all over the world. These people are some of the toughest and most dedicated individuals on earth. I have worked with some of them. I have toured some of their facilities. Law Enforcement gets a bad rap. The public will never be able to appreciate their level of commitment to keeping kids safe from predators. I have known many agents that spend their holidays and days off, thinking of new ways to get the bad guy or chasing down a lead when a sex trafficking victim might be in grave danger.

Yes, crime and crime solving in the future will be challenging. But we are raising a generation of technology geniuses. I know from the training I do in schools that many of those kids will grow up to be leaders that will use technology to change the world for good. They will find unique and effective ways to go after pedophiles and protect the next generation of kids from predators.

CHAPTER ELEVEN:

GLOBAL DARK NET-CHILD PORNOGRAPHY RINGS

THE DARK NET: A SECRET CYBER WORLD WHERE IMAGES OF SEXUALLY ABUSED CHILDREN ARE COLLECTED AND TRADED BY LIKE-MINDED PEDOPHILES WHO FIND EACH OTHER AND DEVELOP A BOND THROUGH SHARED FETISHES OR IDEOLOGIES.

I n early 2012, I began to notice in the research that I was doing on human trafficking that there was an increase in the number of child pornography cases being prosecuted across the U.S. It has been fascinating to watch the trend as seemingly, every day there is a new case of child sex exploitation being reported through social media. My first inclination was that with the plethora of news media, blogs and social media and the availability of news media from around the globe at our fingertips, the number of cases was probably not increasing. Rather more cases were being publicized and were available for reading.

Now I realize that what we are seeing is a convergence of technologies that are allowing pedophiles that normally hide in the shadows to meet on the Internet, share their common fetishes, and exchange Dark Net website addresses. They bond; they feel accepted; they are emboldened. They form large scale underground pornography communities and even divide into sub-communities based on an ideology or fetish.

Take a deep breath, this is hard to hear. Some prefer pre-pubescent boys or girls; some prefer early teens; some like sado-masochistic torture; some prefer infants and toddlers. It is pure evil.

Most of us don't want to know about it or even hear about it. It makes us want to run out of the room and take a shower. I get it. I do. In some circles, they have renamed it so it is easier to discuss publicly.

Sometimes it is called "Child Exploitation Materials" or CAM- "Child Abuse Materials". Renaming it does not change. It just makes the public dialogue a bit easier to communicate.

But I decided early on, that pretending is not going to save these kids. This work is NOT for everyone. One cannot do this work without a strong spiritual foundation and a determination to eradicate this evil. NEVER AGAIN, should another man, woman or child have to endure this kind of evil.

Ashton Kushner, the famous movie star, also leads "Thorn", a nonprofit organization dedicated to developing technology to combat sex trafficking and child pornography. Mr. Kushner provided the following quote. "According to the available data, the U.S. is the largest distributor of child abuse material. Data shows that 9.8 million IP addresses are exchanged for child porn files in the US (11.8 million IP addresses worldwide.)

The U.S. Department of Homeland Security runs an extraordinary program called ICAC- Internet Crimes Against Children. They do not get enough credit for the amazing work that these individuals do to keep our (your) kids safe on the Internet. If you ever meet one of the people who work at ICAC, give them a hug. This is the Lord's work.

According to a Homeland Security spokesperson, "The ICAC Program was developed in response to the increasing number of children and teenagers using the Internet and other technology, the proliferation of child sexual abuse images available electronically, and the heightened online activity by predators seeking unsupervised contact with potential underage victims". I have met many of these individuals and I can fully attest that they have far more cases than they can handle. The sad statement about our society is that we even need a government agency to protect our kids online.

To understand how underground child pornography sites work, you have to understand the configuration of the Internet. In fact, I think this should be a required course for all kids BEFORE they are handed a cell phone. It is these underground Dark Net sites where many of those illicit photos that our kids take of each other end up. This happens because some slick predator cons our kids into sending them a naked photo.

If you think of the Internet as a bucket of water, the top 3%-5% is where we all live our cyber lives. It is called the "Clear Web or Surface Web". We have Google, Chrome, and Bing. We have search engines and IP addresses. We have a means of searching and finding each other. Billions of bits of information are at our finger tips.

Below the "Clear or Surface" Web is the "Deep Web". For the most part, that is where government entities and major corporations store their databases. Finally, the rest of the Internet is made up of the "Dark Net" or "Dark Web". Few people understand just how vast the Dark Net is. While the Dark Net does maintain a basic "Directory", it does not function with IP addresses and search engines. That makes maneuvering through the Dark Net much more difficult. To be successful, you really have to already know a specific web site address to be able to find someone easily.

To be able to access the Dark Net you need a specialized router. There are several routers that are utilized but the most famous one is "TOR" which stands for "The Onion Router". The Tor Router is relatively free to access but you do need a high-end computer to do the set up. What we will often see is kids from more affluent families with more discretionary income are more likely to be the teens that have access to a Tor Router. If you ever see someone using a dot onion (.onion) account, they are in the Dark Net as opposed to dot com (.com) or dot net (.net).

The way pedophiles use the Dark Net is that they will meet in the Clear Web first and find individuals who share their fetishes. Pedophiles recognize many of the graphics and icons that are used by other pedophiles that will suggest they have a specific sexual preference or fetish.

Once they find each other, they hook up and do a kind of qualification of each other to be sure they are not talking to an undercover law enforcement officer. Once they are satisfied the other individual is legitimate and relatively safe, and share their fetishes, they then exchange information on how to access Peer to Peer networks or specific underground child pornography sites. Once you understand the process, then you ask yourself, "Why doesn't law enforcement do undercover stings and take these creeps out?" THEY DO. But it is very difficult work.

Case 1: The Playpen Child Pornography case.

Let me share with you about the Playpen Child Pornography case. On February 19, 2015 the FBI arrested Steven W Chase of Naples, Florida. The FBI had received a tip about a website from other law enforcement officers who had discovered that Chase was operating a child pornography Tor Website which was misconfigured. Once Chase was arrested and incarcerated so he could not alert other Playpen users the site had been confiscated, the FBI took control of the Playpen site.

Let me stop here and share with you a personal "opinion" of this. You may not yet understand what is happening here. THE FBI TOOK CONTROL AND OPERATED A CHILD PORNOGRAPHY SITE FOR 13 DAYS IN THE DARK NET. That is akin to placing an undercover officer in a motel during a prostitution sting and he actually engages in the sex act.

While I am historically a law and order kind of person who strictly follows the rule of law to the max, I am personally proud of this activity. Yes, it was against the law. But for the first time in our life-time, we now understand just how big these child pornography rings are in the Dark Net. Up until this event we had no understanding that we were talking about HUNDREDS OF THOUSANDS of little kids who are being violated all over the world to satisfy the sick and disgusting fetishes of pedophiles.

Our laws and legislation are designed to combat crime in a rule of law and chain of evidence kind of setting. We find a crime; we gather evidence; we get a search warrant; we prosecute a case. Until this event, it was virtually impossible to get a search warrant because you could not prove what you were looking for. No one had any clue the magnitude of the criminal activity involving the violation of children taking place in the Dark Net. Had the FBI waited until there was an organized development of the Dark Net address system to be able to get a specific and defined search warrant for a specific activity, literally hundreds of thousands, probably millions of kids would have continued to be violated.

Once the FBI took control of the Playpen site, they implanted a NIT (network investigative tool), which is Malware, onto the server. For the non-technology reader, just imagine injecting dye into the veins of your body to see where it ends up. They found

Playpen had over 215,000 users and hosted 23,000 sexually explicit images and videos of toddlers and children. It was reported that over 100,000 Playpen users visited the site after the FBI took control of it and the FBI managed to gather evidence on 1300 Playpen users around the globe.

Subsequently, many of the cases of child pornography in the U.S. were thrown out by the courts because the original search warrant was in Virginia and their first case involved a perpetrator in Oklahoma. However, the FBI has continued to advance their Appellate Court cases and they now have an Appellate decision based on the Rule 41, which gives them carte blanche per se, to go where they need in the Dark Net for future cases.

In the end, Steven Chase received a sentence of 30 years and lost his residence and will be on a lifetime of supervised probation if he ever gets out. He was 58 years old so with a little luck this guy will never again see the light of day. Two of his co-conspirators were also sentenced. There have been some very long sentences in the U.S. for child pornographers, but in my opinion there will never be <u>enough</u>.

There are some underlying factors involved in belonging to underground child pornography rings. In many of the cases that I have examined, all members of an underground child pornography ring have to submit a new photo of themselves violating a child EACH WEEK. The pornography ring leader examines many of the photos to check that they are not being photo shopped and watches for law enforcement infiltration into the ring. Think about what that means for a ring like the Playpen ring. With 215,000 child pornographers participating in the Playpen ring, that means <u>every week around the world, 215,000 children are being sexually violated</u> in the most horrific way to maintain their membership in the Playpen ring. That is not just 215,000 photos.

IN ORDER TO MAKE CHILD PORNOGRAPHY YOU NEED A CHILD.
IN ORDER FOR IT TO BE PORNOGRAPHIC, YOU MUST VIOLATE THAT CHILD IN A HORRIFIC WAY.

I have been following the nuances of child pornographers for many years. I have charted their age, gender, race, types of collection (video, photo, live streaming etc.), whether they are just viewers, or they manufacture and distribute. I track their gender and age preferences of their victims. When possible, I track their professions but that is a biased number because we never see a headline "Ditch Digger is a child Pornographer". We only see the headlines for School Superintendent, Pediatrician, Police, Military, etc. That is how the news works. They always want to nail the big fish.

I would really like to get a grant to access all the child predator's legal cases and build total profiles based on non-public data generated by courts and law enforcement. The purpose of this research study would be to try to figure out 1.) WHO and 2) WHY. I have thousands of hours of trying to figure out why this happens, so just maybe we can find a cure for it.

What my cursory research indicates based on PUBLIC DATA (news releases etc.), the most likely profession engaged in child pornography abuse is connected in some way to the school system whether it is private or public. There is no particular position that is utilized by these pedophiles. Sometimes it is the substitute teacher, or teacher's aid, or a full-time teacher, a counselor, a sports coach, a Principal, and sometimes, yes, even a School Superintendent. It seems pedophiles seek out jobs where they have access to children. Following after school professionals are Pastors, Pediatricians, and Police.

The age ranges can vary from teenagers to men who are well into their eighties. Originally, the age range that was most common was 45 to 65 but lately the ages seem much younger. I cannot help but wonder if that has to do with the prolific availability of pornography our young men see through social media and online gaming, but that is shear speculation on my part.

It seems like every day; Million Kids posts a new case of child pornography on Million Kids Facebook page. The proliferation of global online child sexual exploitation is some days overwhelming. It is hard to decide which cases to include in this book. It seems the availability of the global internet and easy access of child pornographers to innocent minors and children that child pornography has become a true epidemic.

Law enforcement agencies are utilizing advanced technologies and innovative approaches to combating child abuse materials in a big way. I am proud of them! Child pornographers are the vilest individuals on earth. While there are days it is hard to report on a large case of abuse or a particularly devasting act to a child, I experience great hope in researching and understanding what technology developers and law enforcement are doing to win the battle against child sexual exploitation. The following case shows some of that innovation.

Case 2: 79 Arrested in New Jersey

The headline read: **79 Arrested in Massive Child Pornography and Trafficking sting" (Tapinto Montclair)** "Operation Safety Net" a nine-month multi-agency child protection initiative, New Jersey ICAC.

Let's take a look at the individuals they arrested and charged. Before I list these, let me emphasize that these were arrests and the charges are ALLEGED. All parties are innocent until they are proven guilty in a court of law. My point here is these individuals come from all walks of life.

The Perpetrators were from all counties in New Jersey and also from California and Indiana. The

perpetrator from Indiana tried to have children transported from New Jersey to have sex in Indiana.

Defendants – Ages 14 to 75.

A camp counselor who allegedly sexually
assaulted a 14-yr. girl under his supervision.

A youth minister who allegedly sent lewd photos
of himself to a young girl.

A 24-yr. old man who allegedly used a phone
app to record underage girls performing sex acts on
themselves.

A Trenton Police Officer who allegedly amassed/
distributed large amounts of pornography

A swimming coach who allegedly amassed/dis-
tributed large amounts of pornography

A piano teacher who allegedly amassed/distrib-
uted large amounts of pornography

An IT Professional who allegedly had over 138,000
files (one million photos).

A mechanic who allegedly had with over
10,000 files.

Three brothers who allegedly had over 5000 files
of child pornography.

The purpose of including this case is just to
emphasize that there is no such thing as a "classic

pedophile". One of the things that always catches my attention is that many of these pedophiles are very disciplined and accomplished individuals. It may be a music director or pediatrician or a law enforcement officer or a rocket scientist. In many of these cases, the individual also has children of their own and many are married. What is really fascinating is that many of these individuals have advanced degrees that required ongoing and intense self-control and self-discipline. Many of those same individuals actually will post the photos and videos of violated children on their work, school or church hard drives or computer systems.

How does that work? Do they just suddenly become temporarily unable to have cognitive reasoning? They must surely understand they will get caught. And yet, their addiction, their compulsive need to exploit, seems to overcome any possible concept of logic and sense of reality.

In looking at this case from New Jersey, there are some real breakthroughs for law enforcement. What was really exciting about this operation is that law enforcement used a new van equipped as a "mobile cyber forensics lab" and a new canine trained to sniff out electronic devices. I get really giddy when I think about the possibilities of this.

First, having a mobile van is like outrageously cool! When law enforcement does a child pornography bust, the perp will go wild trying to destroy devices even to the point of drowning their computer in a bathtub. Having a mobile van at the location provides law enforcement with a major opportunity to stay on the scene and download the data for as long as they need to get all the evidence.

What is really over the top for me, is that these guys discovered that canine units (police dogs) can be trained to sniff out the chemical that is used in the manufacture of thumb drives and cell phones. Think about this, thumb drives often look like Legos, or coins, or key chains or umpteen other things and law enforcement can miss them in a search. The new thumb drive sniffing canine apparently is like a metal detector sniffing out devices law enforcement would never discover.

How cool it would be if every county could afford a canine that sniffs out cell phones and thumb drives in jails and prisons. That might put an end to running child pornography and sex trafficking rings from prison. Way to go New Jersey law enforcement for your ingenuity. I am proud of you!

When I first entered the world of researching child pornography, one of the things that I originally looked at was the number of individuals who possessed photos and videos versus individuals who manufacture and distribute child pornography. My original thinking was that if we could provide mental health counseling intervention with individuals who only "possessed" child pornography, maybe we could save them AND ULTIMATELY SAVE A CHILD.

As I mentioned in Chapter Two, it is very difficult for a child pornographer who is "possessing" to reach out and get counseling. Almost every state in the nation has "mandated reporter" requirements for all mental health and public counselors such as teachers, pastors, priests etc. As soon as an individual reveals they have an interest in a sex act with a child, even if it is just possessing a photo, the professional counselor is mandated to report it to authorities.

Thanks to my relationship with law enforcement, I have sat in on videotaped interviews of pedophiles and charted case after case, in the hopes of understanding what makes pedophiles the way they are.

Many pedophiles will tell you that they were molested when they were a child, but of course there is no way to document most of their claims. When you speak with law enforcement specialists that deal with pedophilia they will tell you that is bunk. Pedophiles are looking for a way out, a way to minimize their actions, and make themselves out to be the REAL victim.

Case 3: Roland Yockel

One of the cases that I followed was the case of Brockport, NY pedophile, Roland Yockel. He was a kindergarten teacher who was sentenced to 13 years in prison and given a $250,000 fine. When he was arrested for child pornography, law enforcement found a vast stash of child pornography in his home. He admitted in court that he struggled with the problem and apologized to the children who were brutally victimized in the thousands of images and videos he watched. It is rare in my experience that a pedophile even realizes that victims were brutalized in order to make those images. There is no way to determine if he is sincere or just trying to minimize his sentence.

A MAJOR concern is that Yockel was a kindergarten teacher and he seemed to have a sexual fetish for children in that age range. He also worked as a recreation counselor in a nearby town and admitted to stealing underwear from some of the children. Law Enforcement found children's underwear under his mattress. He admitted that he once let a child that his mother was babysitting, sit on his lap and he became aware that he was sexually aroused.

In some of the lectures I have heard from pedophilia experts, they believe that most pedophiles are aware of their attraction to children as early as 14 and 15 years old. I have not seen anything to substantiate it, but there is some collaboration to the concept in Yockel's statement based on his experience. There is some indication from the prosecutors that Yockel was conducting online chats about the sexual acts he had fantasized about with youngsters.

According to the article written by Gary Craig, from the Rochester Democrat and Chronicle, while investigators say they discovered thousands of images of child pornography on Yockel's computers and more than 130,000 images of "child erotica", there was no evidence that Yockel sexually abused any children.

Yockel said he never sexually touched or molested children but he did fantasize while watching them at camp. Yockel's attorney stated that in his early 20's he became addicted to adult pornography and "fell down the rabbit hole" of child pornography.

He then started going to online chat rooms where he discovered kindred spirits who would discuss their fantasies. They even role played their fantasies with each other.

The reason I selected this case for this book is the impact that social media played on Yockel's acting out. This supports my argument that time and time again, when pedophiles begin to realize they may have a deviation, a fetish, they then go online and find others with compatible fetishes and the community grows and expands as they reinforce the legitimacy of exploiting and torturing the child.

My point here is the group acceptance seems to deepen the addiction and totally obliterates the reality of the lifetime of pain and suffering they are imparting on another human being, most often, a small helpless child whose life is destroyed forever.

Underground Dark Net groups are one of the horrific aspects of "The Societal Shift". The Clear

Web brings like-minded individuals together where they develop comraderies and endorse each other's fetishes. Once a bond is forged in the Clear Web, they exchange Dark Web addresses and form sub-cultures where even the vilest acts elevate your status in the community.

I often wonder how these pedophiles "find" or "identify" each other. Certainly, you would most likely never go to a dinner party and start a conversation by saying "I am into four-year-olds". The risk of being found out and judged is enormous. But the WORLD WIDE WEB opens doors and makes introductions in ways that could never be possible before the GLOBAL INTERNET CONNECTION.

Where this is headed is totally terrifying. You will see when I get to the last chapter of this book, that I believe the availability and vulnerability of millions and millions of impoverished third world kids and adults combined with technology that can bring together thousands of pedophiles in an interactive conversation while watching a child be violated will be the most prevalent and lucrative money laundering crime of the 21st Century.

Case 4: Conor Emmett

One of the cases I researched was the Conor Emmett case. Mr. Emmett's child pornography case was generated with the investigation of the Playpen case above. Conor Emmett, 20 years old, was arrested after he came to the attention of the FBI and Interpol in the Playpen investigation. One of the frustrations in combating child pornography is the disparity in sentencing around the globe from country to country. In this case Conor Emmett was in the possession of 5919 images and 328 videos at the time of his arrest in Dublin, Ireland.

One of the videos was of an 18-month-old baby girl who endured a sado-masochistic rape and torture at the hands of Conor Emmett. The rape and torture were supposedly saved in still images and videos and sold and traded among the thousands of participants of the Playpen child pornography ring. The abuse was over seen by a woman who appeared to be conducting the violence to the child in Thailand.

At the time of his arrest, law enforcement found a book with the title "Welcome to Paedophilia Handbook" on Emmett's computer. The handbook included sections on "How to handle police and the public if things go wrong", and "How to have sex with kids in safe and rewarding ways", and "When is the appropriate "hunting season".

For most of us, we will alternate between wanting to puke and experiencing outrage that this monster was not locked up for the rest of his life. As a person who lives and breathes to create ways to keep kids safe from these monsters, what is fascinating to me was the lack of outrage at the dastardly nature of the crime. No one seemed to care that the child had not only suffered egregious abuse but that the photos will be circulated to tens of thousands of pedophiles for the rest of her life.

The Judge in this case, Judge Karen O'Connor suspended the last 15 months of a two- and half-year prison sentence. Judge O'Connor noted that Emmett was a good student, has been involved in charity work and has engaged in intensive rehabilitation. Emmett's attorney stated that Emmett had done great work to overcome what was obviously a sickness. She stated that Emmett was from an extraordinarily good family and has parents that have supported him throughout because he is a kind, caring, and loving person. She stated that Emmett did very well at school, completed Gaisce awards and now volunteers at a charity shop. An editor's note- would this be a charity shop where children of all ages come and go freely and are introduced to Emmett without the knowledge of the crimes he has committed? HELLO!!!!!!!!!

Emmett stated that he started looking at child pornography at the age of 16 because it interested him. What is important to the author is that Emmett did NOT self-identify. He only admitted to it when he got caught. And he only got caught because of excellent work on behalf of the FBI in the ground-breaking Dark Web investigation, which we now know as the Playpen case.

One cannot help but wonder how many more innocent infants and toddlers would have been violated without law enforcement intervention. The other critical factor that no one seems to be outraged about is that this court case was based on ONE infant that was violated. But Emmett had images of nearly 6000 cases where children were being raped and exploited. We have no idea who they are or where they are. But as we all know, child pornography is

NOT a victimless crime. In order to make nearly 6000 photos of child pornography, you need at least nearly 6000 CHILDREN and those CHILDREN must be violated or it is not pornography. Sometimes it is difficult for me to maintain my composure as I try to educate the world that child pornography is a dastardly act!

A study of child pornography would not be complete without acknowledging that there are many more female child pornographers than our society wants to acknowledge. If you are a faithful follower of Million Kids Facebook page, you will see a case where a female is convicted of possession, manufacture or distribution of child pornography about once a month. Whenever I educate law enforcement, health professionals, therapists, and first responders, I make a point of discussing this. Just like in sex trafficking, from time to time you will encounter a case where the female is the perpetrator.

Sometimes, it is because the female is being exploited by a male pedophile and they provide their child as a way of either staying relevant or important to their male violator. Sometimes, the female will allow her children to be violated so she gets a reprieve from being victimized herself. Sometimes, it is a mother on meth or heroin who will do whatever they need to do to get their next fix. Sometimes, they use it to lure in a new boyfriend who is also a pedophile. She may provide access to her own children or arrange an encounter with other children whose mother will trust her as a female friend. Regardless, we cannot discount the fact that there are female pedophiles the same as there are male pedophiles.

Case 5: Emily Oberst

Let's look at the case of Emily Oberst who was sentenced to 60 years in a child pornography case that rocked a private religious school in Syracuse, New York. Ms. Oberst and her boyfriend Jason Kopp were convicted of multiple counts of child pornography including the violating of a newborn baby on the night she was brought home from the hospital as well as nude photos of a student taken in the school's bathroom where Ms. Oberst worked. Some of her crimes were against three young children who were extremely young and vulnerable.

The Judge in this case referenced text messages between Oberst and Kopp showing her willingness, even eagerness to engage in sexually explicit behavior with the children. Ms. Oberst' s attorney stated at sentencing that Oberst had a good upbringing in a good home and there was nothing in the defendants background to explain her behavior.

Case 6: Linzi Shifflett

Another case to consider is in Dallas Texas. It is the case of Linzi Shifflett, who was 29 at the time of sentencing. Ms. Shifflett was charged with molesting a 4-year-old minor child who was in her custody. She took sexually explicit photographs and videos of the child. Ms. Shifflett then sold the photos for a nominal amount of money to a man in Florida. In addition to a sentence of 60 years in federal prison, she was ordered to pay $194, 815.17 in restitution to the victim.

Finally, in a discussion about combating pedophiles and child pornographers, I want to share a line of thinking about the libraries that many pedophiles maintain in order to satisfy their addiction.

Over the past several years, massive databases have been discovered containing photos and videos of exploited children. In Scotland, a database was discovered with more than 30 Million images of child pornography. Similar databases have been found in Ireland and Norway. It seems nearly every month we see a new headline in the U.S. that announces the finding of a library of one million or five million photos of sexually violated children. The most recent case highlighted on Million Kids Facebook page contained over sixteen million images of violated children.

When I hear these discoveries and see the headlines, I am always curious what is the reality of this situation for the pornographers. It would be physically impossible to sort through and view one million images in a reasonable length of time, let alone 30 million images. Most of us can barely maintain a photo album of one hundred or two hundred photos. But really, ONE MILLION IMAGES? And yet there is never enough.

These pedophiles buy, sell and trade all day and all night, horrific images of children, babies, toddlers, teenagers and on and on. That is the entire modus operandi of sextortion. They sort them. They categorize them. They label them. They make more photos. They trade and buy more horrific photos. It would seem to me that there is actually a contest. It would appear the larger your database, the more you are "revered" by others in your child porn ring. Perhaps, that is why they lose all sense of reality and begin to store the photos on their corporate databases. In some cases, it has actually been on law enforcement databases, on NASA's database and YES, I AM NOT MAKING THIS UP ON THE VATICAN'S DATABASE.

One of the curiosities I have entertained from time to time, is whether or not all of this will change as live streaming and group pay-per-view live streaming events take over still shots and videos. When you read the final chapter, you will see what I am talking about. Even at this writing, group live streaming is possible. Pedophiles can form pay- per-view (or free) live streaming events where they can come together and chat with each other while they are viewing a child being violated. They seem to bond with each other and share the experience. The sixty-four-thou-sand-dollar question is this! Why would you risk being found and arrested by maintaining a million-photo database, when you can share the experience with literally hundreds of like-minded pedophiles and when it is over, ALL THE EVIDENCE DISAPPEARS because it was live streamed?

I am curious to see if pedophiles continue to maintain their mega databases to prove to others their status and success when they can minimize their chances of being caught by operating only on live streaming. Only time will tell. My bet is their sick and perverted egos will continue to build massive databases because they all believe they are not going to get caught.

CHAPTER TWELVE:

HUMAN TRAFFICKING: GANGS AND SOCIAL MEDIA

Human Trafficking is a phenomenon that has been around for centuries. It is, in essence, human exploitation through labor or sexual abuse that involves force, fraud, or coercion. Certainly, for centuries there has been slavery. The oppression and exploitation are utterly despicable whether it is man, woman or child.

Human Trafficking is the fastest growing crime in the U.S. Polaris Project operates a national hotline where the public can report suspected incidents of human trafficking. Statistics from their hotline indicate that about 33% to 40% of calls were about foreign nationals that may be victims of human trafficking. That means that 60 to 70% of cases of human trafficking in the U.S. are U.S. citizens, many of which are minors who have been coerced or seduced by a boyfriend, girlfriend, or social media.

Million Kids (and I) have been combating sex and labor trafficking in the U.S. since 2010. In early 2012, I was exposed to my first horrific sex trafficking case of a beautiful fifteen-year-old girl. This case changed my life as I very quickly understood just how vulnerable our naïve and unsuspecting kids can get lured in. I wrote about this case in my book "*Seduced*".

What was unique about this case was the victim was from a two-parent household with loving and caring parents. The girl was smart, beautiful and an all-around star. The only mistake she made was befriending an older girl in her high school, who was quick to buy her gifts and build what looked like a solid friendship. However, in this case the girl was a "Bottom girl".

Pimps and gangs often use some of their trusted girls called "Bottom Girl" in the commercial sex business to lure in other girls. These girls may be 17, 20, 24, 48 or even in their 70's with some of the sex trafficking rings I have researched. They will promote the girl and give her some responsibility as a supervisor of sorts. She places ads, instructs the younger girls on sex acts, disciplines the girl and sometimes even handles the money.

What is critical to understand in this scenario is that "Bottom girls" have quotas for a minimum income they must earn each day in commercial sex. The "Bottom Girl" will often recruit younger girls who trust another girl quickly. Then she turns this girl over to the pimp. It is a simple strategy. The girl has a quota and she can either earn it herself or recruit others to earn the money.

Truthfully, on the street, she is called something much more vile and disgusting than "Bottom Girl" but I prefer to not use that language. The challenges of understanding the role of a "Bottom Girl" are many. Certainly, you cannot be a "Bottom Girl" if you have not already been in the life. That means that most "Bottom Girls" started out as victims.

Personally, because I have been in the business of combating sex crimes for many years, I do everything possible to see all females as victims in the crime of sex trafficking. However, it is simply not always true.

Sometimes, a "Bottom Girl" is even more violated than the other girls. A pimp or pedophile may gang rape her or sodomize her to set an example to the other girls so they will not go rogue or try to hide the money. So many "Bottom Girls" are highly abused. However, in many cases the "Bottom Girl" is more violent, more abusive, less forgiving, and more controlling than the actual pimp.

The challenge for Law Enforcement is how to tell if the "Bottom Girl" is a victim or a vicious, manipulative female who will blow your head off with her concealed weapon as you are trying to treat her as a victim. It is not an easy task.

The very nature of the role of the "Bottom Girl" makes it easy for her to access and recruit victims. Most of us think of pimps as a high rolling male with a fur coat, gold chains and rap music. But who would not trust another 17-year-old female student in a high school, especially, if she has the latest clothes, the newest electronics, gets her nails done regularly, and goes out to eat whenever she wants to?

In this landmark case, the "Bottom Girl" was a member of a street gang. She had been enrolled in a local high school for the sole purpose of recruiting innocent and unsuspecting kids. This case was truly tragic as they lured in a beautiful young lady who was trafficked for many months in some of the worst parts of Los Angeles. She was subsequently located and rescued. The case was tried and the eight defendants including the "Bottom Girl" received long and deserved sentences.

Thankfully, everyone in the victim's family are truly extraordinary individuals. They surrounded the girl with love and acceptance. I am certain the recovery has not been easy, but she has done phenomenally. Today, she is married with a child and is truly a walking miracle. Many victims of sex trafficking do not get so fortunate. Her mother has been a primary catalyst in encouraging me to educate as many other young girls as possible about how pimps and predators are lurking in schools with deceptive intent.

However, it was this case that taught me about how gangs and cartels use females to recruit in schools.

Based on that case, our Chief of Police in Riverside assisted me by reaching out to the Superintendent of Schools. They invited me in to train their staff, teachers, counselors, nurses, truancy officers, security staff and school resource officers.

It has been quite a journey as I have now trained tens of thousands of school personnel. Equally exciting, is that many of the staff members have arranged parent symposiums. Even more exciting, is that I have been privileged to conduct hundreds of training events for students. It is through those events that I receive most of my leads on potential cases.

What I find is that if you will be straight forward with students and tell it like it is, for the most part, they get it. Most young people want to be leaders and succeed in life. Most young people do not understand how the Internet works and how pedophiles and predators really operate.

Human trafficking is often a difficult subject for most people to comprehend. For many people, they visualize a scenario that was famously portrayed in the movie "Taken" where the victim is virtually kidnapped. Truthfully, the recruitment is more often a crime of psychology as we discussed earlier.

There are two primary factors in recruitment for trafficking. The first is a desire to be loved, to be approved of, to be accepted, and to belong to someone. The second is a desire for easy money or a willingness to engage in an opportunity to make more money than would normally be available to you. As we discussed earlier, the most qualifying elements of recruitment are AVAILABLE AND VULNERABLE.

The reason that this strategy works so well is that we ALL want those things. Whether you are a lonely housewife, a hormonal teenager, an underpaid male in a third world country, a starving model wannabe, or a teenage boy sexting with a twenty something hottie in a video game chat room, at one time or another, we are ALL vulnerable and available. For the first time in history, we are being brought together with the world's pedophiles and predators, AND THERE ARE NO RULE BOOKS, NO INSTRUCTIONS, NO PHOTO LINE UPS. Nothing is preparing any of us for this historic and global event.

The majority of our society will have close calls and narrow escapes but will arrive at adulthood unscathed by sex trafficking, sextortion, social media exploitation, or child pornography victimization. But for those that are ensnared, their lives will become a living hell. That is why I am writing this book. As I take lead after lead from devastated parents about how their 13-year-old daughter has run off with a 25-year-old pimp or their son is being exploited by an online predator, I believe it is important that parents around the globe understand just how quickly their lives and the lives of their children can change.

There is a wide variation on the types of human trafficking. To understand the concepts of human trafficking in terms of "The Societal Shift", it is important to understand the underlying factors that motivate pedophiles, pimps, and predators and sometimes even gangs, terrorists, and home-grown violent extremists.

We are currently experiencing a worldwide epidemic of sexual and labor slavery. It is difficult for me to convey to an audience just how varied and complex this crime is. Often an organization will invite me to speak and only give me twenty to thirty minutes. What a challenge to convey the true depth and breadth of the issue in such a short time.

Human Trafficking is a complex issue and it has taken on a scale and scope of exploitation that is hard to relate. If you, as the reader, are interested in becoming a speaker or getting involved to become a leader in combating sex and labor trafficking, I will warn you it is all-consuming. I do my work about seventy hours a week and I am always far behind. So often we see a documentary about trafficking or hear a survivor speak and it opens our eyes. But that is simply one perspective and while it is a very important perspective, we all need to remember this is just one variation of the overall complexity of the crime.

What is Human Trafficking? In the U.S Human Trafficking was originally defined by the Trafficking Victims Protection Reauthorization Act (TVPRA) and Congress has since added more components to the law. In essence there are three components to defining Human Trafficking through TVPRA.

1.) **Process**- Recruitment, harboring, transferring, or receiving
2.) **Way/Means**- Threat, coercion, abduction, fraud, deceit, deception, fear, abuse of power
3.) **Goal** – Prostitution, pornography, violence, sexual exploitation, forced labor, involuntary servitude, and debt bondage.

These are abbreviated descriptions of what defines trafficking and how it works. If you have a couple of long, lonely nights bored out of your mind, you may want to research this yourself and follow the trail of legal ins and outs as this has been litigated. But for the average reader, that will help us understand the many ways this takes place.

Labor Trafficking is a global problem and one that we are all trying to understand better in the U.S. Because of the mass migration and refugee movement around the globe, I believe this will become more and more prolific. It truly is a "Societal Shift" as ethnic groups and whole cultures are being uprooted and transplanted in places far away from their homes and all that was familiar to them.

Many of these people have lost virtually everything: their identity, their income, their family surroundings, their possessions, and sometimes their sense of dignity. Add to that fact, obtaining employment that provides an income equivalent to their old life is nearly impossible. Most important to understand is that these folks have lost ALL elements of security and they are forced to take risks in ways they never thought they might do.

As a reader of this book, please keep in mind, this has happened to these people simply because of who they are and where they live at this time in history. Most are good people who are desperate to re-establish their families and live their lives in peace. But homeless and displaced people are prime targets to become victims of sex and labor trafficking.

The stories are in the millions. From time to time a special story appears in a news release, a blog or a video. But for literally millions, their stories are never told.

A friend of mine who works with sex trafficking victims in India told me one such story that has preyed on my heart. They did a mission's trip into Turkey and Jordan and went into a refugee camp and spoke with individuals who had fled the war in Syria. He told the story of a middle age man who had run his own computer repair business in Syria. He was a good family man, who worked hard, saved his money, sent his kids to school, and loved his wife.

As the war advanced and conditions deteriorated, he sent his wife and two daughters to live with relatives in England. He kept his young teenage son at home to help him protect his household and continue with his business. He said he really needed the income from the business to maintain stability for the household and finance his wife and daughters living away. But what was most important to him was his familiar lifestyle, his own set of circumstances, which defined who he was. He stayed because he knew if he walked away, someone would take over his house, confiscate his business, and he would lose everything. He thought that the war might be over soon and if he could just hang tough, they all would survive and the family could return.

As the war expanded and the devastation came closer and closer to his home, with bombs going off nearby, he finally capitulated. He gathered what he could and he and his young teenage son made the escape to a refugee camp in Turkey. My friend visited them in the camp. It was simply too awful to describe. The son was separated from the father because he was a minor. He was placed in a juvenile detention center that was formerly a prison. He was 13 and he was placed with thousands of other juveniles who were mixed with older teens and guards who preyed on the minors. The father was terrified for his son and what might happen to him.

The reason I share this with you in the context of "Societal Shift" is that this story is being played out around the world in Africa, Italy, UK, Germany, Syria, Turkey, Sweden, Myanmar, El Salvador, Guatemala, Afghanistan, and on and on. Think about the loss and desperation these folks experience.

I understand the reverse side of this issue. Believe me I do. When thousands, even millions of foreign individuals invade your country, then your country is also at risk. Traveling with these desperate individuals are thousands of criminal individuals who prey on those in need and living in dire circumstances.

An example of this scenario is the thousands of MS-13 gang members that have invaded the U.S. from El Salvador and are now preying on our young teenagers and adding a gang element to our communities in the U.S. These gangs did not thrive here before the wave of illegal immigration.

There are many fine young people who came in illegally and are an asset to our community. But how can you tell which ones are the good ones and which ones are the bad ones when you have a country with no borders or border control? The purpose of LEGAL immigration is to provide an organized process to bring in quality individuals that will add value to our communities and then eliminate those criminal individuals that will cause harm to our society. Immigration is a privilege; not a right. It is important that we have protocols that follow the law to ensure the safety of the individuals within our country.

As the entire world comes together through technology, it makes me tremble to think about how easily displaced and/or impoverished individuals can be reached and taken advantage of. A good father, a scared mother, trying to protect and support their family will take chances they never would have taken when they were in the security of their community in their homeland. The Internet will enable the most vulnerable to be reached at any time.

Just imagine the scams and employment offers that will be used as a cloak to suck in innocent people desperate to re-establish themselves. The fathers can be welders in the U.S. and make $60,000, and moms can be nannies making $30,000 and the daughters can be models and the sons can be in a rock band and be rich and famous and on and on and on. All they have to do is pay a recruiter $8000, (their life savings) and that recruiter will get them into the U.S. (or the UK, Sweden, France, Italy, Thailand, etc.) and their lives will be good again.

Remember, trafficking, whether it is sex trafficking or labor trafficking is a crime of psychology. A displaced and uprooted individual, a poor family making $3000 a year in Central African Republic or Haiti is a sitting duck for fraudulent global labor recruiting.

Before we judge these folks, I can guarantee you, that if I was in Rwanda or El Salvador, I would be the first to do what I had to do to change my world. But it is that very willingness to take chances that helps us all understand how easy it will be for cartels, organized crime, pedophiles and predators to access, groom, recruit and exploit desperate and displaced people, when we become A WORLD WITHOUT BORDERS.

Next, I would like to address the complex and diversified aspects of gang trafficking in the U.S. I suspect there are similarities globally. I often refer to the Scale and Scope of sex trafficking. When I first started in the business of combating trafficking in 2010, in the U.S., we would see cases where there was one pimp and he was controlling five girls/ women in his stable.

Today, it is not uncommon for our task force to see cases with five or more pimps, one recent case had 22 pimps and literally 20,30,40, even up to a hundred females being exploited. The rate at which this epidemic has expanded over the past several years is simply hard to convey. That is what I mean by Scale and Scope. The cases are larger, the geographical areas where the victims are sold have greatly expanded and the intensity of the abuse is inhumane.

Case: Lawrence Gunn Jr.

As an example, the Riverside County Anti Human Trafficking Task Force (RCAHT) where I serve as the Training and Outreach Coordinator, had a case involving a perpetrator named Lawrence Gunn Jr. He is what we call a gorilla pimp. He was especially violent, beating the girls, giving them a black eye, burning them with irons and cigarettes. For several of the girls, he tattooed his gang moniker "Classified" right down the side of their faces. The physical, sexual, and emotional abuse these young girls suffered is beyond description. It is difficult for the average person to comprehend it. There were 28 victims. Many were

15 to18 years old, who were forced into the most degrading and vile acts anyone can imagine. These girls were recruited out of Southern California and sold into Alaska and Minnesota and most likely many other states.

Whenever I analyze a case like this one, I try to look at it from the perpetrator, victim and law enforcement perspective so we can train others about how all of this takes place. The hope is that this information will assist NGOs and Law Enforcement in how to recognize these patterns and be able to say "Never Again" should another young girl be violated like this.

Just imagine the level of victim services these young girls need. Besides legal assistance and tattoo removal (in some cases plastic surgery), they will have years and years of rebuilding their emotional capacity. Many victims have PTSD, flash backs, night mares, and endless bouts of self-blame and self-degradation. Many have a lifetime of physical damage to their most vulnerable parts and will have anal and oral herpes forever. The women (and men) who overcome this trauma and are able to rebuild their lives are nothing short of extraordinary heroes.

From a law enforcement perspective, our team (RCAHT) did a yeoman's job on this case. Cases such as this require hundreds of hours of investigation and evidence gathering. There are multiple search warrants and multi-state law enforcement agencies. It is a massive effort to assemble testimony, medical history, and psychological profiles for 28 victims.

It is a real challenge to build trust with the victim and even more of a challenge to help her assist with the case and not disappear because perpetrators, even those in prison, can send threats to a victim who might consider cooperating with law enforcement. Just consider what it takes to build a case based on technology evidence such as texts, emails, chat rooms conversations, live streaming, cell phones etc. and assist prosecutors to go to a Federal Court and build a complex and vivid case for a jury.

Remember our society still has a tendency to think of prostitution as a voluntary, independent decision where most people are in it because they want to be. Based on my ten years of working with sex trafficking, there are SOME independent adults but the vast majority are being coerced, directed or controlled by a greedy agent that demands they turn over part or all of the revenue that was generated through the sexual violation of their bodies. Imagine being violated five, eight, ten, fifteen times or more a night and at the end of it all, YOU DON'T GET ANY OF THE MONEY.

In Southern California, 85% to 90% of the cases have a gang nexus. When I say that I can feel parents in the audience breathe a sigh of relief because they believe their child will never join a gang. But don't be so sure. In this day of social media, many kids interact with gang members without understanding what they are doing. I sometimes tease that gangs have IT guys. Well that is a bit of an exaggeration, but truthfully gangs do use social media in ways most parents don't realize.

Before I start into a comparison of how gangs operate sex trafficking rings, let me first say that the most likely targets for sex traffickers are

1.) Foster Kids,

2.) Homeless Kids,

3.) Runaway Kids,

4.) Pregnant Teenagers.

I addressed this in other sections of this book but I wanted to reiterate it because these categories of individuals are the most preyed individuals by gangs. Think about how easy they are to manipulate.

A foster child has often been in multiple homes and has repeatedly been told they had to meet a particular behavior standard to be able to stay. So, when they are 13 and a gang guy tells a foster girl he will "take care" of her but she has to do something in return, it comes naturally to her that it is just how it is.

Statistics provided by the National Center for Missing and Exploited Children indicate that 60% of kids in commercial sex (prostitution) come from foster care and 80% of homeless kids come from foster care. Add to that, many state court systems have ruled that a cell phone is more than a cell phone. It is your bank and your communication to your community. Therefore foster kids and even kids in group homes can and should have cell phones. That is creating an electronic superhighway for access to a child that is very vulnerable. Gangs understand and have a PHD in accessing, grooming, recruiting and exploiting foster kids.

Gangs do not all operate alike. Too often, we as civilian individuals tend to use a broad brush when talking about sex trafficking or even gang trafficking. In reality, there are a wide range of types of modus operandi for gang sex trafficking. It is important that school officials, foster agencies, Licensed Marriage and Family Therapists, youth ministers, social workers and law enforcement understand the differences.

Case: Dog Pound Gang

The Dog Pound gang is a famous case of sex trafficking from Fresno, California. I casually referred to this style of gang as a bunch of "Thugs" versus a sophisticated Cartel style gang. They are what you might think of as a group of young guys who often appear together in groups and flash their wealth and dominance. They would appear in baggy pants with tattoos, hanging chains and flashing gang signs to show their inclusion. Most of the participants were 15 to 25 years old.

They would use their young and good-looking gang members to lure in vulnerable and available young girls from the neighborhood by pretending to be their boyfriend. Think Romeo Pimp. These girls were usually from broken homes, foster homes, were runaways, and even some were homeless girls. The Dog Pound Gang had actually been operating for years, violating young people right under everyone's noses. When Fresno installed a new Chief of Police things began to change. THANK YOU.

These gang members "Groomed" the girls through social media. Initially the girls thought they were part of something important and they belonged to the gang. The gang members gave the girls drugs and also got the girls to sell drugs and promised the girls they would be free and rich.

One point that I think is interesting is that they operated out of an upscale suite at the San Joaquin Hotel. Somehow when we as the public think of commercial sex, we immediately visualize a seedy motel (called Hotel Motel) on the outskirts of town. Not so in this case. Honestly, in many cases the commercial sex is offered in the better parts of town. The girls would be lured in by the boys with the promises of being taken care of. However, once initiated, they were drugged, and often beaten and threatened with death. The gang members manufactured fraudulent credit cards and used the older girls to rip off businesses with fraudulent credit cards for more than $1.45 million dollars.

I do believe this is an important point for all of us to understand. Sex Trafficking is not only NOT a victimless crime, but it affects crime in the entire community and affects businesses and corporations.

Seldom is sex trafficking a stand-alone crime. We know that victims of sex trafficking are forced into a wide variety of other crimes such as credit card fraud, stolen credit cards, stolen vehicles, shop lifting, and drug selling. That is why I value my relationship with high quality corporations that support and donate to our work. These corporations get it. They want to make a difference not only to the young people in our community but they know their corporation can also suffer loss as these crimes expand.

Understanding gangs from the stand point of "Societal Shift" is critical. The Dog Pound Gang used social media to connect with the victims initially; they used social media to manage the activity, to advertise and sell the commercial sex; to control, intimidate and keep track of the young victims. Ultimately, they used technology to process the vast amount of money being made.

The Dog Pound gang was netting $30,000 a week, by selling vulnerable teenagers around Fresno and nearby towns including Las Vegas. When the members of the Dog Pound Gang were arrested, they found $50,000 in cash, and impounded 17 vehicles including a Bentley, Range Rover, a party bus and a boat. All of this wealth was made on the backs of exploited foster, homeless, runaway, and pregnant young people.

But get this! The Dog Pound Gang sex trafficking ring was being run from PRISON. That is right. Their leader, Deandre Stanfill used a cellphone within the prison to run the sex trafficking ring!

To emphasize my point that not all gangs operate alike, let's take a look at another gang operating in Fresno. The Bull Dog Gang was a sex trafficking gang that operated across the U.S.

To compare the two gangs, the Dog Pound Gang members were younger, less sophisticated, preyed on local girls and guys and were funded through fraudulent credit cards, selling drugs and commercial sex. They were something of a street gang that made money and for the most part kept it locally and bought outlandish and frivolous goods to brag about their wealth.

Case: Bull Dog Gang

The Bull Dog Gang was more sophisticated. The members were older with members ages 19 to 52. This is a cartel style gang which generated millions of dollars but used the money to support criminal cartels.

The Bull Dog Gang had an elaborate recruiting tactic by using all styles of apps, chat rooms, dating sites, live streaming and social media and gaming tactics to meet girls and women across the U.S and build a relationship. Social media is a world without borders so they were able to build the trust of women throughout the U.S. including New York, Iowa, Texas and California. Once the girls met up with their social media friend, they were groomed, broken, and sold into forced prostitution. Many of the adults and minor victims were forced to work around the clock. Many were drugged.

This case is a very sophisticated case of a national sex trafficking ring that required collaboration of the FBI, DEA, ATF, and Homeland Security as well as many local law enforcement agencies. Law Enforcement conducted <u>more than 630,000 communications intercepts.</u> Just try to imagine the number of man hours, lost holidays, late night shifts, and back to back weekend duties that this required.

I share those facts with you because these cases are extremely demanding cases to investigate, gather evidence, interview victims and witnesses, and prepare them for court. I can well imagine the kind of extreme violence these victims endured. According to news releases of this case, wiretaps allowed law enforcement officers to stop SIX gang shootings.

If you were a victim who had fallen in love with a guy on the Internet and the next thing you know you are in Chicago being forced to perform sex acts around the clock, and controlled by automatic weapons, you probably are not going to ask for help from your next sex date. You most likely realize at any given time, all you have to do is say the wrong thing, not make enough money, or look like you are going to ask for help and you will either be gang sodomized and filmed, or are facing death in the vilest way. Few of us can appreciate the trauma, the fear, the degradation these victims experience.

Case: Brock Franklin

Let me share the case of Brock Franklin, who was sentenced to 400 years in a Colorado State Prison (THANK YOU, COLORADO!) Franklin was a gang member that used social media, especially Facebook to meet girls online and lure them into prostitution. He was part of a sex trafficking ring that had seven members. Franklin is what we call a gorilla pimp. He controlled by violence and narcotics. Franklin set rules and daily quotas and if you did not make your quota you were severely punished.

Franklin took all the money the girls earned each day. One juvenile girl said she met Franklin online and he convinced her to run away from home. He gave her ecstasy. He would punch her in the face and later caused permanent damage to her eye and ear. Another juvenile victim said that Franklin required her to perform oral sex on other gang members in front of everybody. One of the adult females said that Franklin kept her wired with GPS so he knew where she was at all times. On more than one occasion, he choked her; he pistol whipped her; and he raped her.

When I see these cases, I ask myself "What can I do to stop this?" "How can I change this?" "How can we say never again?"

The bottom line for me is this book.

I know this is hard to read. Thank you for taking this journey with me. As hard as it is to read this (and write it), if we do not educate the public, nothing will change. Just think of the millions of kids and adults around the U.S. and globally that are at risk of meeting a total hunk on the Internet, only to find their dream become a nightmare. We must talk anywhere and everywhere we can; talk often and explicitly. That is why I do what I do.

One final thought on gangs. Because of social media and the "Societal Shift" it may feel like gangs are not as big a threat to our communities as they used to be. You might even ask yourself about when was the last time you chatted with your child or grandchild about not joining a gang. One of the enigmas about social media is that it is changing gang organization. This is a critical factor in the "Societal Shift".

Seldom do you see the large crowds of homies hanging on the street corner. They communicate by social media. They are dispersed. In fact, one of the unique attributes of MS-13 is that it operates in cliques, often out of storefronts. They move into small communities across the U.S. and set up a "franchise" to their home group in El Salvador. To the average citizen, it feels like they are losing influence. Nothing could be further from the truth.

In fact, we are seeing more and more gangs working together in ways they never worked before. Sometimes they join forces for specific operations and then they operate independently other times. Because of social media it is in fact, as we say "A World Without Borders". The idea of controlling a four-block territory is not as prevalent as it once was. Just because you don't see them, does not mean they are not there. Talk to your kids about not joining a gang.

CHAPTER THIRTEEN:

WHO ARE THE SEX BUYERS?

O ne holiday my husband and I were having dinner with family friends and their family.

We were talking about my work and sex buyers. Their middle age daughter suddenly said, "All sex buyers are Caucasians, in suits, and they are all Republicans". Now, I love this young lady and she is normally brilliant. I respect her immensely. She is certainly more intelligent than most people I have met but it was amusing to me how far askew this line of thinking was. My guess is that she had seen the movie "Pretty Woman" and was thinking of all "johns" as men like Richard Gere. Well, nothing could be further from the truth.

Curious about her attitude, I did a cursory research project of Googling several cases across the United States where men were arrested for soliciting the sexual services of commercial sex providers in undercover stings. Often various cities will arrest sex buyers (known as Johns), post their photos in the local newspaper which ultimately ends up on Google.

Certainly, the ethnicity of each male arrested was not identified but based on general appearances in the photos I would say they were equally divided by ethnicity including African American, Hispanic, Caucasian, Middle Eastern and even some Asians. This was also discerned by looking at the individuals' last name and there appeared to be an equal mix of ethnicities. The obvious other issue is that very few of these men were wearing suits.

It is possible that men who buy sex and wear suits might be procuring their commercial sexual services on sites other than the most popular sites known for advertising commercial sex services. Maybe with their college education they have figured out that law enforcement preys on those common sites when setting up undercover busts and reverse stings and they know enough not to frequent those sites.

What I DO know from my work with the Anti Human Trafficking Task Force is that we never ask a person's political persuasions. I share this story to help us all understand our prejudices.

I do have a strong opinion that much needs to be done to educate men about how prostitution has changed. I have often said on my radio shows that men need to be told "This is NOT your father's pros-titution". By that I don't mean to disparage anyone's father. My point is that almost without fail, some male will tell me that prostitution has been around forever, even before the time of Christ. Trust me, I get it. I do. However, commercial sex enterprises have changed dramatically in recent years.

Long gone are the days where a sex provider can operate independently. A few still try, but with social media, gangs, cartels and controlled sex rings it is getting harder and harder to remain indepen-dent. I often think it would be like going to Compton, California or the barrio in Chicago and standing on the street corner and deciding to sell a bag of weed. That will last about 5 minutes when the local gang leaders will show up and make you pay up as that is their territory. The same thing is happening in commercial sex.

Certainly, a woman (or man) can decide they are adults and it is their body and they want to make money by offering their body to anyone willing to pay. However, it is getting harder and harder to remain independent. Some pimp, some boyfriend, someone will show up saying they need to be "Managed" and that is their territory.

And very quickly the sex provider slips from the category of "independent provider" to becoming exploited. Almost always the manager (pimp) gets a cut and before long they are demanding it all. They begin to set quotas or put the heat on them "to do it for Daddy". They start to use drugs. The thought of being an independent sex provider is simply a far-off dream from a better time in their lives.

You will often hear me say, that in case after case that I have examined, never once did the victims have any ability to visualize the path they were about to go down or the devastating end they would find in their lives. I hope and pray with the thousands of hours of education provided by Million Kids and other fine organizations, we will open the eyes of naïve girls and guys and save them from being violated.

So how should society deal with sex buyers? We all agree that without demand there will be no need for a supply. Most people who bring up this subject have little idea of the complexity of the issue. Again, just like my fine friend, they have a naïve and uninformed point of view about prostitution and sex buying based on Hollywood or some politician on trial for philandering with prostitutes.

I believe that educating men is critical to changing the demand for commercial sex. But that is not the ONLY solution. First, before you walk away in disgust believing that I am some starry eye idealist, let me share with you the thinking that has caused me to arrive at this conclusion.

In my research, there are primarily three categories of sex buyers.

One is gang trafficking where the victim is passed around from gang member to gang member and also offered to the public. Frankly, no amount of education is going to stop those sex buyers. The only solution I can see is to support your local law enforcement, equip them with the latest technology (gangs use technology for recruiting and selling), support your SWAT teams with equipment and then go hard after them with laws, arrests, prosecutions, etc. Additionally, there are community programs that are successful in educating and intervening with young potential gang members so they will not get recruited. It is important for those young people (both girls and guys) to understand how gang sexual exploitation works so they will not become members of gangs. Once they are "sexted" in and are gang members the males will become sex "payers" for victims of gang trafficking.

The second category of sex buyers that few people are aware of and most of us don't want to look at is sex buying in the migrant trafficking scenario. Many times, when females are brought up from foreign countries (primarily Mexico and Latin America for the U.S.), the migrant girls are forced to service large numbers of migrant workers each day. Additionally, many of the migrant workers owe money to a Coyote, a labor recruiter, or a Cartel and the exploiter will "encourage" the migrant to go in and have sex with migrant girls being held in Casitas at the end of the day.

The purpose of this is for the Cartel to keep both males and females in bondage and use any monies earned by laborers to be returned to the Cartel by coercing them to pay for sex in a Casita. The price usually runs $15-$23 for 15 to 20 minutes. The girls being held in the Casitas are true "sex slaves" and many of them never survive the long-term effects of this desperate situation. It is truly death by sex.

In this case both the sex buyer and the sex seller are being exploited. The only real means of dealing with this type of sex buying is for Law Enforcement, the Department of Labor, Immigration, Border Patrol, Department of Agriculture, and other agencies to join forces and implement and ENFORCE strong immigration laws in our country and develop extensive financial penalties and long sentences for the Coyotes, Cartel and illegal labor contractors. Unfortunately to date, our country does not seem to have the stomach to enforce the existing laws, let alone develop tougher laws that might stop the Cartels from buying and selling sex in our communities.

The third category is "Joe Sex Buyer". The average guy wants to get laid. He may use dating sites and commercial sex websites, pornography sites, and live chat rooms to hook up or even visit an illicit massage parlor. Commercial sex is also sold at truck stops, residential brothels and often at large scale public events such as the Superbowl, electronics conventions, and rock festivals, that bring in thousands of partying young people. This category I believe has some hope of being changed once most of the men understand the issue.

I would agree that there are some men (and women) in the world that are not redeemable. No matter how much education, how many arrests, how much public shaming, they will not change. Also, there are some men and women who are into bondage, sadomasochistic violence, extreme fetishes and feel they have a right to purchase a willing partner in a financial transaction. The reality of that is that few of the men and women who are engaged in sex trafficking have any voluntary say in these transactions. These women and men are horribly violated and are forced to engage in despicable acts. If our society cannot find a means of making this totally illegal and bringing these people to justice then we need to search our souls. A society which cannot or will not protect victims of sexual abuse, is a lost society.

But I am just optimistic enough to believe that the majority of men "Joe Sex Buyer" category will change if they understand what is taking place in the world of commercial sex. It is this category that I believe will benefit by education about the new world order of "prostitution as usual".

I often use my AM Radio show "Exploited: Crimes and Technology" to help the public understand the issue. I want them to know that if they are responding to an ad on the Internet or other commercial sex advertising site that two things are happening.

First, the commercial sex business is now controlled by cartels and organized crime or their local gang. If they are seeking sex services on these sites, they are exposing their family, their wife and kids, to organized crimes. They need to know that if crime rings are willing to provide them with a 14, 15, 16, 17-year-old girl for their pleasure, that those people will take a photo of them with the girl and for a few thousand bucks they won't tell the boss or the wife.

Additionally, the idea of "To Catch a Predator" or reverse stings is alive and well.

Vice squads and Anti Human Trafficking Task Forces, get up every day in the hopes of running a reverse sting and catching these guys in the act, especially if it is a sex buyer seeking a young girl, or an adult female that they can highly violate. Most of the reverse stings end up arresting 5 to 20 men in a very short period of time. They arrest them, book them, take their photos and then put their photos on Facebook. They also become part of the local newspaper article about the sting. So, it becomes VERY public very quickly.

Many District Attorneys and Law Enforcement agencies in Southern California are now buying billboard ads and putting the sex buyer's photo on billboards to help the public understand that sex trafficking is not a "Victimless" crime.

In all honesty, I am a bit uneasy with this tactic although I also support my task force by publishing the photos on Million Kids Facebook page. Let me explain my position on this.

I believe that California or other states should invest in a massive education campaign about sex buying. People need to know that commercial sex has changed and it is very dangerous.

First, they need to know how the recruiting process is taking place and that most of these girls (and guys) that are being advertised are not there voluntarily. This is the work of Million Kids. This is why my first book was titled "*Seduced: The Grooming of America's Teenagers*". Secondly, most of the people being advertised on Internet commercial sex sites were people who never once thought they would end up selling their bodies on the Internet. Many are drugged. And if you look carefully at the photos you will see they are "Branded", meaning they are tattooed with a pimp's name, logo or moniker.

This education is very important because at one time or another most of us will serve on a jury. When the jury pool meets on a sex trafficking case, someone is sure to say "Hey, this girl is alone in a motel room with a John. If she did not want to be there, she could ask for help". Once the public understands that these victims have been duped, broken, disgraced, threated, violated in the worst way and then drugged, they will begin to understand that the victim is simply incapable of asking for help. Additionally, few sex buyers will really assist someone they are paying to violate.

I ask you to think about something else. Just imagine what happens when a John has sex with a commercial sex provider and does not pay her. She has just been raped! More important when she returns to her pimp without the money, her very life is in danger. He will accuse her of stealing the money. In most cases the consequences are extremely violent. Gang rape, gang sodomy, electrocution, burning with an iron, and other types of torture are used to set an example to other girls and make it clear to the victim that she must never again return home without ALL the money.

Men and women in our society need to understand the sex trafficking process. This girl

(occasionally a boy) is being controlled. She may even be drugged. Traffickers withhold food from sex providers to control them, they gang rape them and gang sodomize them. These behaviors make the victim "appear" compliant. She is afraid to ask for help because they are probably threatening to kill her family. It is important that all of society understand the difference between independent sex providers and sex trafficking victims.

Perhaps I am a Pollyanna. It is very possible, although with ten years of research on sex trafficking I doubt it. I do believe that most sex buyers would think twice if they really understood that they were the ninth client that day and just last night she was slapped across the face and gang raped by a group of pimps.

Looking at the sex buyers in the third category, I believe that if many of the men who have been arrested for sex buying of a minor or a trafficked victim, were previously educated about what is happening in the commercial sex business and that the majority of sex providers are being abused, exploited and trafficked, they may think again before buying. Assuming that these are self-serving narcissists that don't get that, then make it clear to them that if they are arrested they will become famous. They will have their photo on a billboard or Facebook page or a newspaper. Perhaps even some of the most hedonistic sex buyers might think twice if they realize their lives are about to be influenced by organized crime, or that they could serve felony-based sentences in prison for underage sex, or they are publicized in their community for their arrest.

The reason that a massive education program for sex buying is so important to me in my fight against sex trafficking is that I do not want to have the efforts

to stop sex buying result in bringing on more victims. I believe that if a man is driving his 14-year-old
daughter and 16-year-old son to school and Dad is
on a billboard for his arrest for sex buying, then we
are about to create two more victims. That kind of
public shaming for teenagers is lifelong. Even worse,
they will most likely be ostracized at school for the
crime of their father.

Many activists will respond with "Well the Dad,
should have thought about that before he did it". And
I don't disagree with that. But that does not overcome the fact that we now have two more innocent
victims that have now entered into dealing with their
father's shame based sexual experience. They will
be ridiculed at school and may be publicly ostracized
for their father's actions. It would seem to me having
a very public education campaign would go a long
way to diminishing much of the demand in the third
category.

There is also a mitigating factor that few sex
buyers want to consider. Today, most escort and sex
services operations are conducted by gangs, cartels
and organized criminal organizations. It is all about
the money. On average, one pimp will control at least

five commercial sex providers. Each sexual services provider usually will generate about $300,000 a year in commercial sexual services in California and they will not be allowed to keep the money. That means each pimp is generating about $1.5 million in income for cartels and gangs. Think what that means to the sex buyer. If a gang or cartel will provide an adult sex buyer with a sixteen-year-old for his pleasure, they will be happy to film that sex buyer having sex with an underage minor and for a few thousand dollars they won't show it to the wife or boss. IT IS ALL ABOUT THE MONEY.

I often am asked "What if prostitution is legalized"? Will that stop sex trafficking?

It is my opinion that it will exacerbate the problem. Look at the cities that have legalized prostitution. Sex Trafficking has not diminished or disappeared where prostitution is legal. In fact, I would argue that many more victims are transported to the area to meet the demand. I believe that legalizing sex will simply create a sex tourism enterprise. It will increase the demand for sex services as it draws individuals that normally would not go to that destination.

The idea that government can now regulate sexual enterprises seems askew to me. Yes, there may be free testing for STD's and more education to the sex providers. But I cannot fathom that organized crime, cartels and gangs will walk away from the enormous financial gain that comes from commercial sex. Additionally, as you will note from other chapters of this book, I believe that much of sex trafficking and commercial sexual exploitation will take place online through pay per view live streaming so cities who legalize commercial sex will become headquarters and safe havens for organized crime but not benefit financially.

Money laundering is usually tandem to sex trafficking, so organized crime can move millions of dollars off shore without paying taxes. Most likely cities and states that vote to legalize prostitution will benefit only with a small amount of proceeds as much of the billions of dollars in income currently being generated through sex trafficking enterprises by organized crime is being moved underground and very little of it is disclosed where taxes are paid to a government agency.

Finally, I want to point out that when a man goes online to buy commercial sex he may not fully understand the risks he is placing on himself and his family. Take a look at this headline: "Prosecutors cleared to seek death penalty in slaying where victim baited by escort ad".

This story is reported by Marc Freeman in the Sun Sentinel. According to the article, Jefty Claude Joseph, Lamart Christophe, and Koral Benshimon were arrested in the slaying of Gustavo Mora Cabral. Cabral responded to an escort service ad listing by "Belle Ayrab Barbie/Sexy Angeline Latina" featuring services that would ultimately be provided by Koral Benshimon. She advertised herself as "looking to have an amazing time".

According to reports, Cabral called Benshimon several times before arriving at the parking lot of the Super 8 Motel. Benshimon testified that she advised Cabral that her price was $100 for an hour and for him to come up to room 226 in a few minutes.

When Cabral entered the room Joseph and Christophe were waiting and ordered Cabral to the ground at gun point, tied him up and took $400 in cash, credit cards and his phone. Cabral was so scared he could hardly talk and his life was threatened unless he provided his debit PIN and complied with demands to call his credit card companies to increase his spending limits.

Christophe and Joseph then forced Cabral at gunpoint into the backseat of his black Toyota Camry for a ride to several banks in attempts to withdraw money. Benshimon followed in another car and was later advised to wait for them outside Christophe's mother's residence. A witness told deputies that the three men entered the abandoned house and minutes later there was the sound of a gunshot. Only two men left the house. Police caught up to Joseph and Christophe in the same neighborhood. A search of Joseph's pockets yielded the Super 8 motel room keycard and two of Cabral's credit cards and driver's license.

Benshimon admitted to setting up Cabral to be robbed by Christophe and Jefty Joseph. Cabral ended up being shot in the head in the garage of an abandoned Lake Worth house, though it's not clear who pulled the trigger. It is reported that he died immediately.

That is a tremendous price to pay for a short sexual interlude. Most men can't bring themselves to admit the danger they are putting themselves and their families in when they decide to purchase commercial sex.

CHAPTER FOURTEEN:

FUTURE CRIME- WHERE IS THIS HEADED?

As technology progresses we will begin to see the line between fiction and reality being blurred. I suspect we may already be there for our kids.

This is really an important consideration as we think about the future as it relates to gaming. The first part of this book had to do with how total strangers can access, groom, and recruit our kids through social media apps, live streaming, chat rooms etc. But think about how on-line gaming companies are altering reality for the next generation. It is getting to the point that many young people spend more time in the world of gaming than time with family, church, or even school. People you have never even met and will never meet are laying the ground work for public beliefs.

As I write this, there is a public dialogue going on about who is responsible for making sure that news is truthful and accurate. As the dialogue about "Fake News" continues there is a very disturbing trend taking place. Facebook is beginning to monitor all of our posts and they are deciding which ones are true and which ones need to be taken down. The problem with that is that Facebook are known liberals in their political leanings and there are starting to be hundreds/perhaps thousands of complaints that Facebook is making their censorship decisions based on their own biased and liberal thought processes. Now it is coming out that Google, Instagram and Twitter are doing the same.

This trend means truth has been traded in for censorship based on who is the biggest, the most powerful social media player at the time. This is an important discussion. Already when a news story comes out and you are amazed at the headline, you can channel hop and follow the story. The challenge is that while the players' names are still the same, the story on the various news channels have nothing in common. There is no truth in news anymore as news reporters cross over to opinion, editorial and blogging.

I find it interesting that no matter which channel you watch, they will combine a news fact with an opinion so that individuals cannot tell what is accurate. This is about to get even more difficult for our kids as Facebook introduces the Fayteq technology they purchased in 2017. As we have stated ad nauseum, there are many good uses for this technology and there is nothing wrong with the technology itself but the potential for misuse is mind boggling. This technology will allow users to alter images midstream for instance in live streaming. You will reportedly be able to add images into live streaming and take images out of live streaming while it is broadcasting. Why is that an issue?

Think about the last time you saw a video of a law enforcement officer being charged with using excessive force. You look at the video and sure enough, you can see no reason for that cop to be beating on the man. But then you see a different video from a different angle and there it is, a gun hidden between them that they are fighting over. But the public dialogue goes for the first scenario because it instills anger and emotion and supports a particular cause. When image altering technology arrives, it will be a completely different world. If we cannot believe what we see with our eyes, the truth will be a lost and rare commodity.

I also believe that "Cyber Sex on Demand" or what I call "interactive pornography" or literally webcam sex will be the greatest crime in the world by 2020. Think about what is driving this.

Already sex ads offer out "video viewing" subscriptions for $20 a month. If that ad generates ten new subscribers a day, that is $200 a day or $6000 a month. If the pimp that is controlling that sex provider has five girls in a stable, that means he is making $30,000 a month. He has not risked STDs, he does not waste time driving a girl to the motel, he does not pay for a motel, and he does not risk being arrested in reverse stings by law enforcement.

Well you say, that is better than prostitution where a girl (or guy) is being physically violated. But wait. How can you make webcam sex without an individual engaging in sex acts? In the cases I have seen of forced webcam sex, many of these victims are forced to perform sex acts seven days a week and eighteen or twenty hours a day. That is abuse. The line has already blurred between voluntary pornography production and forced webcam sex.

Let's consider what is about to happen when two technologies converge. When interactive live streaming which has the ability to draw a large audience is combined with the ability to do financial transaction processing, we will take interactive web cam sex to a whole new level. It is inevitable that teenagers (God forbid, maybe younger) will voluntarily perform twerking and stripping in their own bedroom when Mom is not home to pick up a few extra hundred dollars per week. They will simply hook up to Live.Me, Periscope or other live streaming services and start the show. If you don't believe me go to "YOUTUBE" and put in teens twerking. These kids already have a large following.

Our kids already have Bitcoin accounts. They already understand the power of live streaming better than parents. It will only be a short time until live streaming will be commercialized allowing the exchange of credit cards and Bitcoins. Talk about a global supermarket to open the door for commercial sex for our kids. And they never have to leave home.

More important, I believe we will see whole warehouses of individuals sitting in front of webcams producing interactive pornography. By 2020, the entire world will be connected by Internet. All over the globe we will see poor young people being forced or coerced to sit in front of webcams and be violated or violate themselves, so a cartel or organized criminal enterprise can bill billions of dollars which will be laundered through legitimate businesses. In countries like Cambodia, Thailand, Myanmar, Haiti and others, most people are living on $5.00 or less a day. For $8.00, an older brother will set up his little sister in front of a webcam and they just doubled the family income for the day.

Already the selling of children in webcam sex is a ONE BILLION DOLLAR business in the Philippines. Amazingly, that does not seem to be getting a lot of attention.

It is even taking place on U.S. soil. As an example, let's look at the case with the headline "Hungarians use the web to lure gay men into U.S. turn them into sex slaves".

This case dates back to 2014 and it caught my attention because it was the first time I had seen a webcam sex case that was generating tens of thousands of dollars. Additionally, it was a particularly egregious case of abuse. Since the time of this case, we have seen many webcam sex cases and unfortunately it appears to be the way cartels and organized crime will make millions of dollars in the future.

In this case Gabor Acs and Andras Janos Vass from South Florida were business partners and lovers. Their corporation was Their Never Sleep, Inc. Their strategy was to use social media and employment ads in their home country of Hungary to lure gay men to the U.S with the promise of jobs. The victims were promised jobs as hair dressers in New York. Some of the victims understood that they would be doing "escort" work but were never able to visualize the nightmare they were walking into.

Upon arrival into the U.S. the male victims were transported to Florida. According to the article written by Local10.com their lives became an incredible tragedy. I appreciate the reporting done by Local10.

com because few media outlets gave this story the visibility it deserves.

According to this article by Local10.com the victims were forced to perform sex acts in front of a webcam and engage in prostitution for 18 to 20 hours a day. A Federal Agent was quoted as saying "Their traffickers used various techniques to keep them enslaved, including isolating them from others, withholding their travel and identification documents, and using financial manipulation to keep them in constant debt. The victims never received a dime of the money paid for their sexual services.

Ads were placed on gay websites like RentBoy. com and Planet Romeo.com calling the victims "honey boy" or "hot boy". They charged $200 an hour for prostitution services. The agreement was that they would perform sex in front of webcams or have sex with clients and they would turn all the money over to their pimps. Supposedly the victim would get half but their debt would be deducted from their earnings. They were always in debt. That is called "Debt Bondage". The victim will end up owing their captor more than they originally agreed even after weeks of horrible exploitation because the captor continues to expand what they owe them. They will bill them for transportation, food and their bed and living space.

The predators used verbal and physical abuse to control their victims. One of the captors once said "I will kill you all" and threatened one of them with a samurai sword. He would tell them "I will make you disappear: like you never even existed". The victims believed the captors could hurt their families back home. And the victims believed it because they had provided their captors with the family information when they applied for Visas to come to the U.S.

In the end, authorities believed that the three men were billing $40,000 a week for their captors just by providing webcam sex for twenty hours a day, seven days a week!

I cannot fathom the impact on the victims. How does a man survive that physically or emotionally? To my knowledge there are not safe houses to provide services at that level. It was THIS case that opened my eyes to the lucrative nature of web cam sex. Once cartels and organized crime understands that three men equal $40,000 in untaxable money, it will very quickly become their crime of choice.

The case of Hungarian men opened my eyes to the kinds of travesty the victims of webcam sex will be forced to endure. These crimes will be hard to locate and isolate for law enforcement. In webcam sex the victim seldom is allowed to leave the facility and therefore, it will be difficult to interact with someone to ask for help.

Recently I saw a presentation by the FBI and Philippine Police about combating webcam sex of small children in the Philippines. That really confirmed for me where this was headed. As a I mentioned above, it is believed that webcam sex, where little kids are placed in front of a camera and someone around the world is directing an adult on how to abuse them IS NOW A BILLION DOLLAR BUSINESS just in the Philippines. As you are about to see with the onset of pay-per-view interactive live streaming, this industry is about to explode around the globe.

In August of 2017 an article appeared on a German website "Bundeskriminalamt BKA that discussed a case where fifty men paid $7500 each to participate in a pay-per-view webcam sex event. The indication was that these 50 men talked to each through the pay-per-view event while they directed a toddler (supposedly in the Philippines) to be violated as they all watched.

That immediately got my attention. Think about this. If you have 50 men paying $7500.00 each for a short interactive live streaming event, then a cartel or organized criminal enterprise just made $350,000 in underground money and they never delivered a gun or a drug. In a short time, probably ten or twenty minutes, they pocketed a huge amount of money and no one will ever know about it but the perpetrators and the poor child that was violated.

CYBER SEX ON DEMAND, WEBCAM SEX, INTERACTIVE PORNOGRAPHY, INTERACTIVE LIVE STREAMING OF ABUSE WILL BE THE MOST LUCRATIVE CRIME IN THE WORLD BY 2020. Mark my words!

CHAPTER FIFTEEN

WHAT CAN I DO TO MAKE A DIFFERENCE?

F irst, THANK YOU for taking the time and emotional investment to read this book. It has been by far, the most difficult undertaking of my lifetime. I suspect it was also a difficult read for most of you. However, we simply cannot look away and pretend none of this is happening. With over a million kids being trafficked each year and over three million U.S. teenagers involved in sextortion, it is critical that we stop and acknowledge the reality of the "Societal Shift". Then, we must prepare ourselves to educate others and support the least of those among us. Here are some suggestions that might appeal to you if you wish to change the world of sexual exploitation.

1. Let's put the family back in family. Mom and Dad sit together and develop a strategy for a deliberate approach to building a solid foundation as a family. By the time kids are teens, all too often a family has become grand central station where people pass in the night. Decide to change it. Select two nights a week and "put the phone away". Yes, YOUR phones too. Every one's phone goes in a metal box with a lock. Then take the box with the phones to the trunk of your car and lock it away so no one can hear it. It will seem VERY weird at first but it is worth it.

    Have a Barbeque or have the family cook together, maybe even have a theme. Get the kids to cook and share their recipes. Prepare for in-depth conversation if your children are old enough.

    Share with your family how important everyone is to each other. Talk about their talents, and what you like about each other. Tell your children and spouse how proud you are of them for something they have recently done.

Remember when it was a big deal to be part of the "Larson" family (or whatever name your family carries). Put the pride back into being part of the family unit. This is important because when a pimp tries to recruit a young girl or a predator seduces a young guy, the first thing they do is try to villainize the family and separate them. Make it very hard to do.

2. Create a calendar of physical activities. Go to the beach, hike in the mountains, or wildlife park. If you kids are younger, play baseball, or hide and seek. Take walks together and talk. Enroll your child in Taekwondo or a self-defense class. If your kids or grandkids play soccer, baseball, or other activities, go and WATCH them and cheer them on. Mom and daughter may want to take a drama class together so young people can experiment with different identities. Go cycling, jogging or

walking together. Physical activities build confidence and make it easier to bond if everyone is relaxed and having a good time. This is especially important if you believe others are influencing your child on the Internet. The more normalcy they can experience in a safe and casual environment, the more likely they will be to share if they are being seduced or sextorted.

3. Don't be intimidated. Get involved with your child's technology. If there is a father, grandfather, husband and there is a child on a video game that has a chat room, GET YOURSELF AN AVATAR. OK, you may be lousy at it but play a game with the young person so you can understand the purpose of the game and talk about it with family members. If there are issues in the game that are disturbing, discuss it. How do you feel when you kill a cop in the game? There is a lot of sexuality and I am concerned. Who are we talking with? It does not have to be a male that does this but especially if there is a son in the family, it helps

them to bond and also discuss the issues in a non-threatening manner.

4. Get involved with foster youth and homeless youth. If you are a church group or non-profit, there are many activities that can be done to make a difference. First thing is to find the right connections in your community. Are there Independent Living Organizations that help teens when they are transitioning out of foster care? If you find them, meet with them. Can you do a cooking demonstration and give them a small gift of utensils for when they get an apartment and share your recipes? Can your youth group music group come to the foster group home and put on a small concert of inspirational music? Perhaps you can sponsor an independent living youth and help them decorate their first apartment, or help them with a scholarship. Perhaps offer to provide a sports uniform or dance outfit etc. for a foster youth. Have your church hold a parent symposium for foster parents, single parents and grandparents raising grand kids and give the

book "Seduced: The Grooming of America's Teenagers" as a gift. Offer them counseling at no cost or reduced fee.

5. EDUCATE – EDUCATE- EDUCATE. Follow Million Kids on Facebook. Go to WWW. Eploitedcrimes.com (listen) where there are over 100 free podcasts on many subjects including sex and labor trafficking, sextortion, social media exploitation and child pornography.

6. Impact: Your Place in History. Help Million Kids create a documentary that will be distributed free to schools and parents across the nation. The documentary will help young people understand how the Internet is constructed and how predators and pedophiles use social media and online gaming chat rooms to exploit young people. To learn more about this contact: Opal@MillionKids.org.

7. Contact Million Kids at Opal@MillionKids.org for a presentation on sex trafficking and social

media exploitation for your corporate or civic organization

8. REPORT HUMAN TRAFFICKING
   1-888-373-7888
9. **DONATE TO MILLION KIDS. We cannot do this work without you. THANK YOU FROM THE BOTTOM OF MY HEART.**
10. **REMEMBER: The four most powerful words on earth.**

I BELIEVE IN YOU!

REPORT HUMAN TRAFFICKING

1-888-373-7888